The Art of the Horror Film Press Advert

ALRAUNE to ALIEN

1918 - 1979

Paul Sutton

Introduction

Having grown up in the North West of England, during the time of real film and real print, and senselessly strong censorship and very poor film distribution, I accidentally amassed a collection of film magazines so big it can be described as *impressive* or *insane* depending on your point of view. Young and old film scholars in England needed a big collection of print because it kept one connected to world film culture, the heart, legs and much of the head of which had been cut from view by the censors and the flour mill magnates who controlled film exhibition in Britain (in the same way that fizzy drinks merchants and oil companies ran the industry in the States). The stills and the adverts in *Films and Filming, Starburst, Film Comment, Fangoria* and the like, kept us sane.

Then came the miracle of VHS and, for a few short years, every corner shop in Britain became a wonderland library of Fulci frights and Alex de Renzy porn. Then the mainstream bit back with new censorship and new restrictions and it was back to the magazines. A near two-decade wait began for the internet and the IMDB and the customs-charged imported DVD. Then came the downloads. So what's a man to do with his magazines?

The idea for this book, and for the whole series of books that are following large in its wake, in hardback and in colour, came when I made one of my increasingly rare visits to the place masquerading as a three-screen arts cinema in Cambridge. It now shows only the same three files of computer-generated American blockbuster fodder playing at the same time in the two multiplexes in town ("But we're showing a dvd of *The Producers* for one show only on the smallest screen next month. £15.50 for a ticket. Thirty minutes of car adverts before it. Have a postcard!"). Being the grumpy old man that I am, I took pleasure instead in scowling at what passes for film posters these days, all art and design-artistry lost. Having a degree and a photoshop package has replaced the analogue design requirement of having an eye, a hand and a brain.

The golden days of the film poster are often remembered in print and at the auction house, but the newsprint adverts for film are a vanishing breed. There's more art and pleasure to be had from looking at old film adverts than in viewing new film posters in those coffee and junk food *units* that used to show real films.

The "Arts" cinema listing on my birthday in 2018. The very same films were also screening from morning till night in both of the city's multiplexes.

Showtimes at Cambridge Arts Picturehouse

All times are in United Kingdom Time

lay	Tomorrow	Mon, 17 Dec	Tue, 18 Dec
All times	Morning Afternoon Evening Night		

Spider-Man: Into the Spider-Verse

10:30   13:30   16:20

Fantastic Beasts: The Crimes of Grindelwald

11:15   17:30

Bohemian Rhapsody

15:45

RKO ORPHEUM
FREE PARKING AFTER 6 P.M.
3rd HORRIFYING WEEK!
Not Since Los Angeles was a pueblo has it seen such a sensation!
AN EPIC OF TERROR!
FRANKENSTEIN
MORE EERIE THAN LAST WEEK!
By Popular Demand...Another
MIDNIGHT "SPOOK" SHOW
TOMORROW NIGHT
11:30 P.M.
Ghosts...Weird Noises...Strange Lights!
A TWO HOUR REIGN OF HORROR!
[No Advance in Prices]
with BORIS KARLOFF
COLIN CLIVE   MAE CLARKE
JOHN BOLES
A UNIVERSAL PICTURE
Directed by JAMES WHALE
25 TO 1 PM
DOORS OPEN 9 A.M.
NO ONE SEATED DURING FINAL REEL
NO CHILDREN'S PRICES
NURSES IN ATTENDANCE

SOUTH PARK DRIVE-IN 584-4073
LAKEWOOD DRIVE IN
4 SCARY HITS!
DUSK TO DAWN SHOW!
COME EARLY AND STAY LATE!
First Run!
Nocturna
GRANDDAUGHTER OF DRACULA
FROM TRANSYLVANIA TO MANHATTAN...
SHE'LL GET UNDER YOUR SKIN!
If this one doesn't scare you...
PHANTASM
EVIL DOES NOT DIE
IT WAITS
TO BE RE-BORN
THE MANITOU
HE CAME HOME FOR HALLOWEEN
EXTRA BONUS AT 1 P.M.!
A FOAMING CUP OF VAMPIRE VENOM
—IF YOU DARE!

CINEMA WEST
1 BLOCK WEST OF ELLIS & LYNCH   355-4451
WSLI RADIO PRESENTS
A WEEKEND WITH VINCENT PRICE
PG
TRIPLE FEATURE!
6:10 "PIT AND PENDULUM"
7:45 "THE RAVEN"
9:25 "DR. PHIBES"
TODAY AT 5:25-7:20-9:15
KUNG-FU ACTION!
DRAGON VS DRACULA

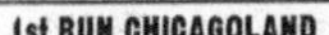
1st RUN CHICAGOLAND

Starts TODAY
FRIDAY the 13th
ALL OVER CHICAGOLAND
THE BLOOD-BROTHERS OF HORROR AND TERROR!
TOGETHER IN THE MOST TERRIFYING MONSTER SHOCK SHOW OF THE YEAR!
ALL NEW! NEVER BEFORE SEEN!
SCARS OF DRACULA
starring CHRISTOPHER LEE with DENNIS WATERMAN JENNY HANLEY CHRISTOPHER MATTHEWS
TECHNICOLOR (R) A Hammer Production for Anglo EMI Distributed by Continental Films
BOTH IN SPINE-TINGLING COLOR!
HORROR OF FRANKENSTEIN
starring RALPH BATES KATE O'MARA VERONICA CARLSON and DENNIS PRICE
TECHNICOLOR (R) A Hammer Production for Anglo EMI Distributed by Continental Films

TAKE CARRIE TO THE PROM.

Who will survive and what will be left of them?
"THE TEXAS CHAINSAW MASSACRE"
3:15
5:00
7:15
9:00
COLOR   R
A BRYANSTON PICTURES RELEASE

CINEMA WEST
355-4451
STARTS TODAY!
ADULTS $2.50
6th SMASH WEEK!
R. 7:45 9:25
HALLOWEEN
TOURIST TRAP
7:35 9:15
PG

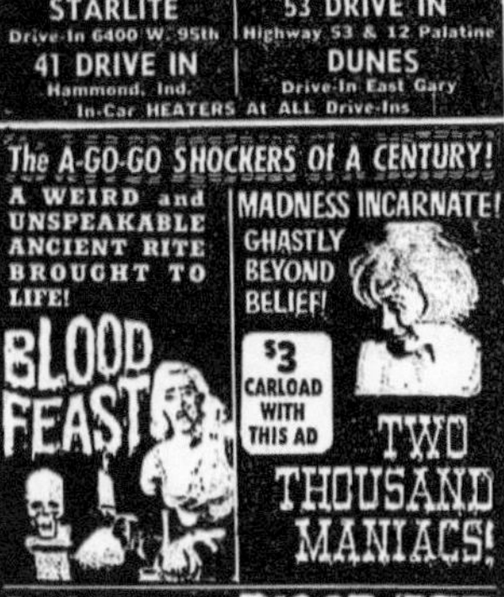
EXCLUSIVE SHOWING AT THESE SHOWCASE THEATRES!
STARLITE Drive-In 6400 W. 95th
53 DRIVE IN Highway 53 & 12 Palatine
41 DRIVE IN Hammond, Ind.
DUNES Drive-In East Gary
In-Car HEATERS At ALL Drive-Ins
The A-GO-GO SHOCKERS OF A CENTURY!
A WEIRD and UNSPEAKABLE ANCIENT RITE BROUGHT TO LIFE!
MADNESS INCARNATE!
GHASTLY BEYOND BELIEF!
BLOOD FEAST
$3 CARLOAD WITH THIS AD
TWO THOUSAND MANIACS!
COLOR ME BLOOD RED

OGGI al REPOSI in prima mondiale
il nuovo gioiello del terrore
NON ABBIATE PAURA. E' SOLO UN FILM. PER ORA...
Titanus
...quando non ci sarà più posto all'inferno
i morti cammineranno sulla Terra...
DARIO ARGENTO presenta
un film scritto e diretto da
GEORGE A. ROMERO
ZOMBI
La proiezione del film è ad «alta fedeltà» con il suono stereofonico a 4 piste magnetiche
Orario spettacoli: 15-17,30-20-22,30
Vietato ai minori di 18 anni

The Art of the Horror Film Press Advert: Alraune to Alien
© Paul Sutton, 2018, 2019
978-1725944206

Second edition
For educational use

Published by Buffalo Books
camerajournal@hotmail.com

Also by Paul Sutton

Understanding Gary Numan
Talking About Ken Russell
The James Dean International Scrapbook
Gary Numan, An International Scrapbook
The Lemon Popsicle Book
The Moving Picture Boy Gallery
The Moving Picture Girl Gallery
Becoming Ken Russell
Charlie Ellis and the Day Trip to Mars
Six English Filmmakers
Remaking Heaven (Sam's First Day)
Lindsay Anderson, The Diaries

Also by Buffalo Books

Paul Dufficey: The Art of Collage
To Each His Own Dolce Vita by John Francis Lane
Falling Upwards by Tim Dry
Ken Russell's Dracula

I've scanned the choicest cuts from my print ad collection, restored them to what could be called *tattoo readiness*, and published them here, black-and-white lovelies preserved for all-time. Some are barely borderline horror films but the genre is a broad church, its door and members are always open to strays and strangers.

Knowing that everyone who picks up this book will probably know all there is to know about the chosen films, and are only a thumb-twitch away from IMDB and its brother demon, Wikipedia, I've not padded out the book with plot summaries and cast lists. I have though included the name of the director and the producer. The producer's influence is often underestimated.

I have added a paragraph or two of text at places where I've seen fit, and aimed to keep my comments informed and original, i.e. as far from Wikipedia-land as I can. On occasion I have drifted off into memory to add a few threads to the tapestry of analogue film-going history, and because to do so links to the theme of the specificity of the print ad. Many of the ads were made for specific screenings at specific cinemas. Long gone most.

For this second edition I have improved the sections on silent cinema and the Universal horrors and bought in a splendid hoard of print ads from Germany, mostly from Munich's Constantin-Film and Nuremberg's *Phantopia-Filmprogramm*. The best of these additions are from the 1950s-1970s when *krimi* was laying the groundwork for Italian *giallo*. German distributors were a major co-financier of the international horror film from the Edgar Wallace chillers and the Barbara Steele frighteners to the Dario Argento spectaculars.

Included too are more scans of swooningly rare original release ads, including ones for such mainstream masterpieces as *Planet of the Apes* and *The Devils*, a pre-release ad for *Dawn of the Dead*, and trade ads trumpeting the box-office marvels of Lon Chaney's *Hunchback of Notre Dame*, Whale's *Frankenstein*, Carpenter's *Halloween* and Craven's *The Hills Have Eyes*. In addition, I have also bitten the bullet and included a lovely load of newspaper adverts culled from American digital collections such as *Held Over!*. These ads aren't as high a quality as scans from my print source originals but they shine a loving light into our film-going history and are too good to ignore.

Paul Sutton, 2019

The Films

The Filmmakers

The Players

The Horror Print Advert Gallery

I vampiri, 1957 d. Mario Bava, Riccardo Freda

Alraune und der Golem (1918)

Print adverts rarely match up to their promises, so I will begin with an advert for a film that does not exist and which never existed. Doubtless it was produced to attract pre-sales and investors, a trick taken up in the 1980s by the now-becoming-cult Cannon Films. The history of cinema is littered with the broken dreams of print promises of films that never got past the script stage, such as Ken Russell's *Dracula* (1979).

The image of the towering demonic figure looming dark and large over the landscape had been a staple of art for centuries, often as a way of representing God and the supernatural. In England, for example, it was the founding template of much of William Blake's art. The image became a staple of the horror advert, particularly in the wake of the mighty promo stills for *King Kong* (1933), in which the giant gorilla stood four times higher than New York City, and in Japan with *Godzilla* (1954). Godzilla was a response to fears of nuclear armageddon after the A-bombing of the country to bring the curtain down on World War Two. The Golem here, looming over the landscape in a Germany locked, battered and losing in the First World War draws on images found on German war posters of the day, and is probably saying to would-be patrons: 'You think it's bad living in a war zone? Just wait until you see the terrors we have created for you!'.

Der Januskopf, 1920   d. F. W. Murnau p. Erich Pommer

The Cabinet of Caligari, directed by Robert Wiene, gave us Conrad Veidt as the eerie somnambulist stealing a maiden across leaning rooftops and jagged painted backdrops that symbolised the broken mind. In doing so Wiene and Veidt, and their designers and crew, brought *German Expressionism* to ten thousand film study courses. There is expressionism aplenty in this ad art for Veidt in *Der Januskopf,* directed by the first master of the genre.

The expressionist leaning shapes on the advert show the influence of Picasso's Cubism. The tortured distorted figure of Veidt as the head of Janus is a harbinger of the Degenerate art that would so upset the Nazis in the 1930s that they took to filling the streets with their repost, aim and fantasy: *Olympian body* statues. The Olympian body approach to public art took its time to filter into the horror film and it did so best from an unexpected source - England's Hammer studios. Hammer's supporting casts of perfectly-formed women enabled the films to do what the Nazis couldn't do - they conquered the world.

Alas, *Der Januskopf* is a lost dead film - destroyed by the leeches living off the work of Robert L. Stevenson who sued for infringement of copyright, the script's main source being Scotland's *Dr. Jekyll and Mr. Hyde.* Ireland's *Dracula* provided the spark, plot, characters and images, but not the style, for Murnau's first living masterpiece: *Nosferatu* (1922). The leeches living off the spoils of Bram Stoker's work also sued, won, and ordered the film to be destroyed. Goodly pirates and bootleggers saved the day by making and preserving illicit copies.

Nosferatu, 1922 d. F. W. Murnau
p. Enrico Dieckmann, Albin Grau

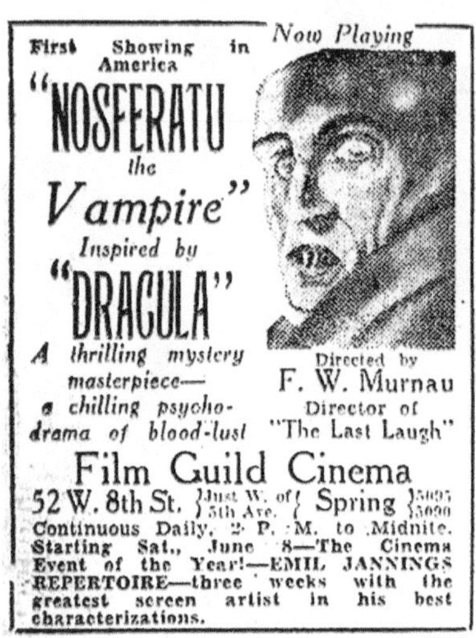

Dr Jekyll and Mr. Hyde, 1920 d. John S. Robertson   p. Adolph Zukor

The Hunchback of Notre Dame, 1923 d. Wallace Worsley p. Carl Laemmle

Look at that incredible American-made set of Paris's Notre Dame Cathedral! Kenneth Clark's landmark 35mm BBC TV series, *Civilisation* (1969) begins with the famed scholar looking at Notre Dame Cathedral, his symbol of a definition of Civilisation. He defines "Civilisation" as having a sense of permanence. Without permanence we are only barbarian tribes moving from place to place, leaving nothing of our selves behind. Four out of the first eight films in this book don't exist anymore; a fair approximation of the percentage of films lost or in critical danger of being lost. Chaney's *Hunchback of Notre Dame* is one of the survivors but, for all its fame and successes, exists only as 16mm reduction prints (and digital scans thereof).

Advertised in Australia as a Sherlock Holmes-style mystery and not as a horror film.

London After Midnight, 1927 d/p Lon Chaney

These ads for the most famous of all lost films are taken from a digital collection. Ironically, the biggest danger to our film heritage came in the first years of the 21st Century in the rush to digitisation. This was partly done as a sort-of preservation attempt to capture a ghost of the films images and sounds and to reduce distribution costs (a 70mm print of *Ben-Hur* weighs more than 300kg). But it soon became apparent that the digital-rush was something of a scam. Digital projection and storage systems have to be replaced every very few years and the quality is still a long way behind 35mm. Compare the lifelike image depths and colour range of any 1970s film shot on Kodak stock, with Panavision lenses, with any digitally-shot film made now. Digital colours are so crude and unlifelike that reduced colour or monochromatic colouring, teal-sheens and yellow-sheens, have become the new normal. They're as far from 'life' as newsprint cartoons. In the 'restoration' of real films, revisionist colouring has become prevalent, particularly in Italy. In the States, censored digital copies, e.g. *if...* (1968) and *Altered States* (1980), now shorn of scenes of nudity, have established themselves as reference copies.

Phantom of the Opera (sound version) 1929
d. Rupert Julian, Lon Chaney, Edward Sedgwick, Ernst Laemmle, Frank McCormick p. Carl Laemmle

Was that a deliberately naughty ad-line? Ad-men do have the loosest morals. The 1925 silent film was re-issued with approximately 40-minutes of new talkie-and-music footage directed by Ernst Laemmle and Frank McCormick.

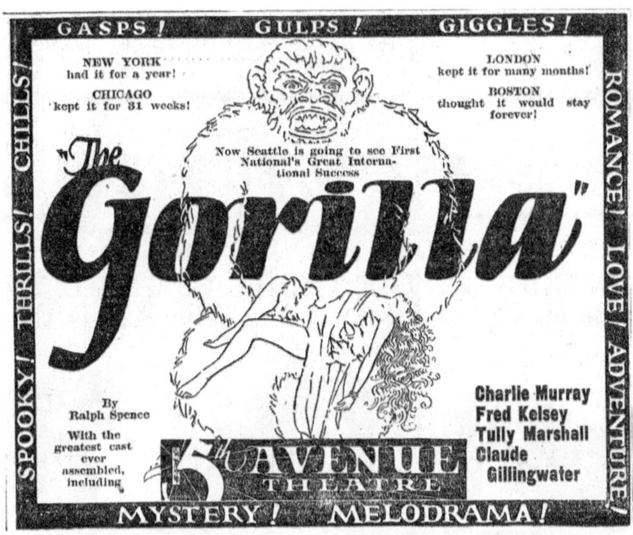

The Gorilla, 1927 d/p. Alfred Santell

A real live gorilla wasn't seen in the West until the decade after Darwin published his shocker, *Origin of the Species*, whereupon live captures were exhibited in London and Paris to gasping frightened crowds. The juxtaposition of the powerful humanoid beast with the fragility and beauty of a woman became a favourite theme of artists in all media. *The Gorilla* was adapted from a Broadway murder mystery play by Ralph Spence. Doubtless 'inspired' by Edgar Allen Poe's *orangutan* chiller, *The Murders in the Rue Morgue*. A hit in its day, the ad tells us *The Gorilla* ran for a year in New York, 51 weeks in Chicago. But it's a lost film. Remade in 1930 and 1939.

Congorilla, 1932 d/p. Martin E. Johnson

1950 re-release ad for the pre-Kong documentary about
'the Big Apes and Little People of Central Africa'

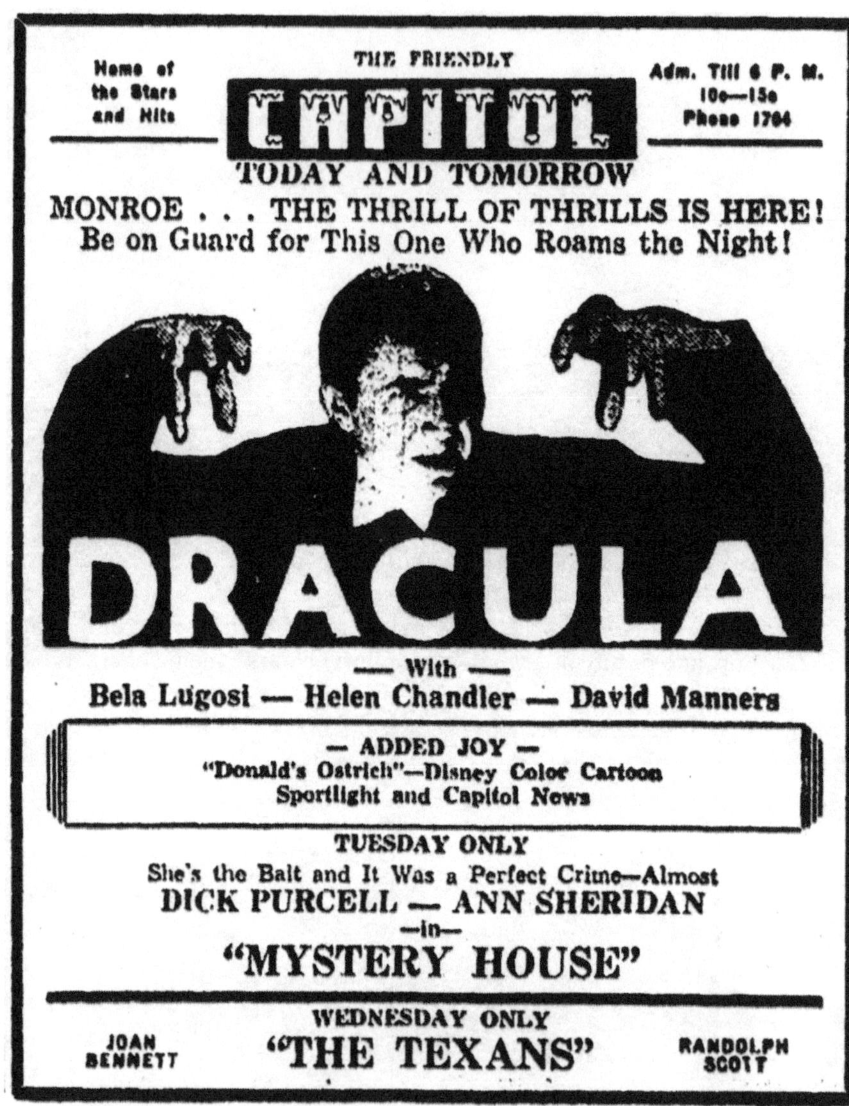

Dracula, 1931 d. Tod Browning p. Tod Browning, Carl Laemmle Jr.

Lugosi's star performance, all enunciation, deportment and stillness, is so richly entertaining, so easily imitated and so impossible to match, it will never go out of style. On stage, Lugosi *was* Dracula upwards of 600 times from Broadway (1927) and Los Angeles (1928) to ... Leicester and Derby (1951). On film he played a caped vampire often but only officially Count-ed twice, bowing out with *Abbott and Costello Meet Frankenstein* (1948).

THE MILLION DOLLAR FACE

CHICAGO
Absolute smash
beating "Dracula"
3rd WEEK
DETROIT
MILWAUKEE
WASHINGTON
HOLD OVER
BOSTON
CLEVELAND
AKRON
FORT WAYNE
PROVIDENCE
GRAND RAPIDS
LOWELL
DES MOINES
SOUTH BEND
**WRECKS
"DRACULA"
RECORD**
ST. PAUL
NEW ORLEANS
OMAHA
SEATTLE
TACOMA
BIRMINGHAM
MEMPHIS
MINNEAPOLIS
LAWRENCE
OKLAHOMA CITY
ATLANTA
PORTLAND, ORE.
DALLAS
SALT LAKE CITY
KANSAS CITY

Critics Rave
"Holds you spellbound"
        N. Y. American
"A dandy … guarantees
satisfaction" N. Y. Daily News
"Most gripping of all"
        Detroit Daily Record
"Unequalled spectacle"
        Boston Traveller
"Terrifying, fantastic,
thrilling" Boston Post
"An epic of screen real-
ism" Boston Daily American
"The ultimate in thrills"
        Boston Globe
"An amazingly effective
photoplay" Hollywood Herald
"This thriller tops them
all" Hollywood Screen World
"Everybody shivered
and had a good time"
        Detroit Mirror
"'Dracula' is mild in com-
parison" Detroit News
"It will entrance you"
        Baltimore Post
"Tops all thrillers"
        Washington News
"One of the best"
        Page Review Jr. Club
"Monstrously exciting
picture" Washington Herald
"May be viewed with
happy alarm by anyone"
        Washington Star
"Charged with electric-
ity" Washington News
"Will quicken the pulse
of the most blase"
        Washington Post
"Will hold you from be-
ginning to end"
        N. Y. Evening Journal
"A singularly fine picture
        N. Y. Eve. Telegram

BREAKS EVERY KNOWN RECORD

FOR FRIDAY, SATURDAY AND SUNDAY, AT MAYFAIR THEATRE, BROADWAY, NEW YORK . . .

FRANKENSTEIN
THE MAN WHO MADE A MONSTER

UNIVERSAL'S SUPER THRILLER   Presented by Carl Laemmle

Frankenstein, 1931 d. James Whale   p. Carl Laemmle Jr.

I don't know where, when or *if* an uncut 35mm print has ever been screened in Britain, but *Frankenstein* wasn't shown uncensored in the UK until Sky Movies Gold (a satellite TV channel) added it to their rota in November 1996! CIC released the uncut film on VHS in April 1997. The five cuts ordered by the UK censors, and news of the Sky screenings, are detailed by Brad Stevens in *The Dark Side* magazine, no.63.

Doctor X, 1932
d. Michael Curtiz
p. Darryl F. Zanuck

Two Technicolor whodunit horror films starring Fay Wray and Lionel Atwill. The first is by the producer-director team who would give us *Gone with the Wind* and *Casablanca*. Bogart himself starred in the sequel, *The Return of Dr X* (1939). The second was co-produced by Hal Wallis, the *Laurel & Hardy* impressario.

Lee Tracy is the wise-cracking reporter in *Doctor X;* Wray the wise-cracking reporter in *Wax Museum* (she even teases a cop with *"How's your sex life?"*). It's as if Curtiz and Zanuck didn't know whether they were inventing the screwball comedy or spoofing *The Front Page* (1931) or *Frankenstein.* Wray describes Atwill's *Wax* fiend as "makes Frankenstein look like a lily."

Both films are amply produced and employ the new technologies of colour and sound, with *Wax* boasting perhaps the noisiest New Year's Eve party on film. It's a fair fun film that's now mostly known for being closely remade in 3D with Vincent Price in the Atwill role. Monica Bannister is the 'dead beauty' prototype for the Laura Palmer or Caroline Munro *Phibes* role.

Alas, *Doctor X,* adapted from a then new hit show on Broadway, is mostly remembered for providing a few fun lyrics for *The Rocky Horror Picture Show*, whose Tim Curry even does a great big 'X' on the press ad (qv).

The Mystery of the Wax Museum, 1933
d. Michael Curtiz, p. Hal B. Wallis, Henry Blanke

The Mummy 1932 d. Karl Freund, p. Carl Laemmle Jr.

This 'INCONCEIVABLY THRILLING! advert for a landmark film takes us back to Broadway and, in the supporting feature, to Hal Wallis's most prized assets. Horror and comedy have always been comfortable bedmates. But the only laughs to be heard in the auditorium when the Karloff film plays are ones escaping from nervousness. It's still an enjoyably effective frightener.

White Zombie opened at London's Dominion Theatre (above) in November 1932. That's the 2,858-seater where *Star Wars* played in 70mm; the Queen musical *We Will Rock You* ran there for a decade. The ad below, from 1939, tells us that *White Zombie* was in circulation the whole decade long.

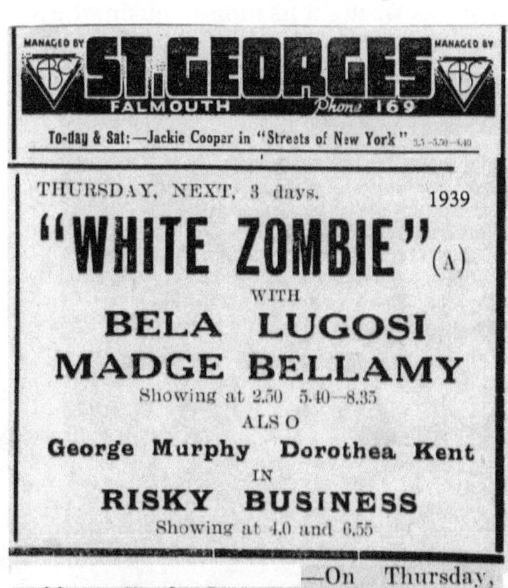

—On Thursday, Friday and Saturday 'White Zombie' will be screened. Madeline Short arrives at Port au Prince to marry Neil Parker, who works in a bank, but on the ship she had met Charles Beaumont, a plantation owner, who prevails upon the young couple to be married in his home. Upon their arrival Madeline and Neil learn that there was an ulterior motive in his invitation. A gripping drama with should not be missed.—Also, 'Risky Business.'

My goodness, what a fantastic advert from France. *"Sensation!"* doesn't do it justice. *King Kong* is a film with many perfections, starting with a perfect story by Edgar Wallace, yes THE Edgar Wallace whose London crime novels would be the foundation stone for German *krimi* and Italian *giallo*. O'Brien's direction and Ted Cheesman's editing give us a perfection of pacing once Skull Island is reached. There's a perfection of casting in Fay Wray; a perfection of imagery exotic, horrific and spectacular. The images of Kong atop the highest man-made point on Earth, with a woman in his hand, and mighty modern planes spitting bullets and causing rivers of simian blood to flow, is so impressive and so loaded with conflicting emotions and layers of symbolism that the giant ape's fall becomes something of a Planet of the Apes re-telling of the myth of Icarus (the inversion of which in 1968 would see the cine-land Moses himself kneeling in the sands of the same city and damning us all to Hell), all fused of course with the fairytale fable of the Beauty and the Beast.

It's a great great film. It's so good in fact that its long shadow still lightens the expensive remakes, such as Dino De Laurentiis's earnest and impressive 1976 re-imagining; Peter Jackson's wholly enjoyable but strangely forgettable 2005 version, and the chop-choppy chopper 2017 reboot, in which the makers amusingly fuse elements and imagery from *Apocalypse Now* and *Cannibal Holocaust* and get a 12 (child) rating! I watched *Kong: Skull Island* in 3D and then in 70mm to pay my respects to the Double Gold contribution to the cinema made by the original *King Kong* producer, the visionary genius, Merian C. Cooper. In 1953, Cooper won for all-time the argument for real film and real picture palaces by giving us Cinerama, and from Cinerama, the cheaper, lesser, but more lasting reduction - 70mm, from which was wrought its junior cousin, the Son of Kong if you will - Cinemascope.

Awe-inspiring newsprint ad for the New York
City premiere at Radio City Music Hall

King Kong, 1933 d. Willis O'Brien p. Merian C. Cooper, Ernest B. Schoedsack

The Bride of Frankenstein, 1935 d. James Whale p. Carl Laemmle Jr

Karloff's performances as the man born without a soul, because he was made by the hands of man and not from the breath of God, are among the finest in all cinema. Under James Whale's direction and Jack Pierce's make-up, he acts-through-the-mask to convey an almost full range of human emotion, from curiosity to loneliness and from gratitude to rage and to fear. The template for this was The Man of a Thousand Faces, Lon Chaney, but the Karloff-Pierce-Whale creation bit deeper into public consciousness.

A reason for that is that Karloff's performance strode further from the styles of theatrical acting that tie much of Chaney's work to the *commedia dell'arte* and to the Victorian theatre. Karloff's was palpably new.

As the decades rolled and rock music and Pop Art were born, Karloff's unhuman monster, with the stiff body and the dark starring eyes, and that alluring combination of wounded fragility and dangerous strength, would be taken up across all areas of performance art. Lanchester's bride had less of an impact because the characterisation was less complex and therefore less open to interpretation, but it continues to make its mark. That vivid lightning strike through artificially raised hair was clearly the spark for Ziggy Stardust.

The spark for this famous re-release was a triple-bill, which included *King Kong*, that opened at The Regina-Wilshire Theatre in Los Angeles on August 5, 1938. The programme drew such crowds that the films played all day and all night and Bela Lugosi was hired to host screenings. Universal pulled the triple-bill after four weeks by which time five hundred new prints of *Dracula* and *Frankenstein* had been struck and the horror double-bill was enshrined as the best night out. Nowhere was this 'Victory' better symbolised than on 42nd Street in New York City for which the advert on the left was placed. A hallowed paradise of art and sleaze, 42nd Street prospered almost to the end of the analogue era.

The advert on the right tells us that the films appeal crossed racial boundaries in The Segregated Land of America, so much so that the 1970s would welcome forth blaxploitation spin offs.

The national success of the *Dracula-Frankenstein* double-bill took exhibitors breath away and blew it into the Universal Studios production meetings. *The Son of Frankenstein* now went into production.

Sequels often have splendid ad-lines.

Friday the 13th was always the day to open a horror film. Orpheum in Seattle was a 2,700 seat beauty (knocked down in 1967).

Son of Frankenstein, 1939 d/p. Rowland V. Lee

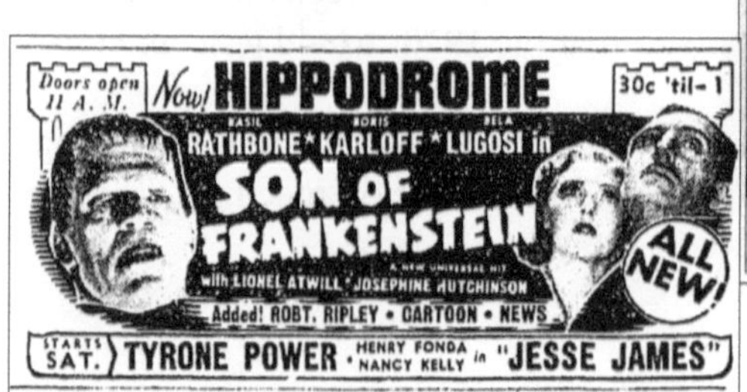

The Corpse Vanishes, 1942
d. Wallace Fox
p. Jack Dietz, Sam Katzman

A bride dies at the altar. Her body is stolen from the Forest Mortuary by a dark-suited Tall Man with a hearse and a dwarf. Yes, we're in inspiration-land for *Phantasm* (1979), but that's as far as it goes.

Four brides die at the altar (three off-screen) and a clue arrives with the fifth in the form of a rare orchid, thus bedding in a symbol of two special sub-genres: the German *krimi* and the Italian *giallo*. That said, this is mostly a smart-woman talkie. A society journalist, a *Ninotchka* hat and pearls performance by Luana Walters, turns detective, and hitches to The Lugosi House - all sliding doors and candles. There's less logic and more bedroom hopping than a Summer season at Blackpool, but hypnosis horticulturist Lugosi and his gang, who include a violent aristocratic wife searching for eternal beauty, bring enough strangeness to deliver the chills.

Angelo Rossitto plays the dwarf henchman. He made twelve films with Lugosi but is best remembered as the villain in *Mad Max 3*.

The advert cleverly downplays all the film's originality and actuality by suggesting to the reader what the ad-man knows they really want, another *Dracula* film.

Frankenstein meet the Wolf Man, 1943 d. Roy William Neill p. George Waggner

Depending on how you score the Universal monster movie series this is Frankenstein 5 Wolf Man 4, or Lugosi 5 Chaney Jr 4. It's of particular note for being the film in which Lugosi played The Monster. He doesn't get much screen time (appears after 35-minutes) but does manage a couple of good fiendish yells. There's a lot to admire here, particularly the photography and the art direction, the camera roving high over the Welsh Talbot graveyard in the opening scene, but too much happens off screen. A goodly doctor tracks Talbot across Europe by press reports of the Wolf Man's killings (none of which we see). All ends with warnings against Mob rule, machines and eco-power. Though made in the midst of World War Two (which adds bite to the attack on machines) it could now be read as an anti-Snowflake horror film.

I Nearly Married a Witch, 1942 d/p. Réne Clair

There are witches, wicked ones too, but this is not a horror film. I include it because the advert is gorgeous. Like several of the best adverts in this book it is taken from the French journal, *Midi-Minuit Fantastique*. *I Nearly Married a Witch* is a mainstream American film made for Chaplin's United Artists by France's most Chaplinesque director, René Clair. Clair's films are characterised by bright anti-Establishment humour and a big fun workshop of in-camera tricks. Revived in high society after being burned at the stake by Puritans, a wicked witch (Veronica Lake, sporting era-defining hair) avenges herself by falling in love with her accuser's 20th Century descendant, a top political candidate on the eve of a loveless marriage. The bewitching begins with the burning down of the Pilgrim Hotel...

I Married a Monster from Outer Space, 1958
d/p. Gene Fowler Jr

I Walked with a Zombie, 1943
d. Jacques Tourneur p. Val Lewton

"It's easy to read the thoughts of a newcomer. Everything seems beautiful because you don't understand. Those flying fish, they're not leaping for joy. They're jumping in terror. Bigger fish want to eat them. That luminous water. It takes its gleam from millions of tiny dead bodies. The glitter of putrescence. There's no beauty here. Only death and decay. Everything good dies here, even the stars."

"The glitter of putrescence" is a great phrase from the second scene in the film (a boat ride taken in form from Lugosi's *White Zombie*, and which we will ride again with Lucio Fulci). It can be used to describe the appeal of the horror genre, but this gently-paced literary film of sibling rivalry, repressed passion, hot winds, distant drumming, calypso singing and a much too rushed finale, is not a horror film. That said, it does provide the defining image of the 1940's horror film: pop-eyed Darby Jones mute and impressive in a dark night field of giant grasses. Jones is the peeled-from-the-rubber-suit forefather of Bolaji Badejo and Kevin Peter Hall. Frances Dee is hired to look after a somnambulist bride on a Caribbean island where voodoo and science have an uneasy alliance. Her room is lined with slattered wood shutters. One shudders with pleasure at how the set and setting would inspire Fulci.

Phantom of the Opera, 1943
d. Arthur Lubin p. George Waggner

It's interesting to note that the Foster-Rains *Phantom* forgoes horror for 'Music Drama' and a gentle romance. A prototype thus for the Brightman-Crawford musical version of the 1980s which proved to be the most popular of them all.

Revenge of the Zombies, 1943
d. Steve Sekely p. Lindsley Parsons

I do like the design (left): a zombie shadow with what looks like a shotgun hole blasted into its head. Alas, we'd have to wait until the fourth wave of Zombie films (after the Hammer and Ossorio-Grau eras) for the great Uncles Tom and George to make good with it. The ad below is the world's first movie-bill of Nazis and zombies long before Peter Cushing made *Shock Waves* with the ex-kid from *Flipper*.

Abbott and Costello Meet Frankenstein, 1948
d. Charles Barton p. Robert Arthur

It starts with An American Werewolf in London telephoning Bud and Lou's delivery office in the States and telling them not to release two crates to a local sideshow owner. Thus begins the very best horror comedy until David Naughton stripped off and started stretching (with due nod to the laughs to be had from *Carry On Screaming*). The script has lines sharper than a Wolf Man's teeth. Lou Costello's genial balletic buffoonery is so skillful here that it went unmatched by Lou's most famous follow-ons, John Belushi and John Candy. Though to the Costello template Belushi brought anarchy and Candy added empathy.

Creature from the Black Lagoon, 1954
d. Jack Arnold   p. William Alland

I'm told by those in the know, for I have not seen them myself, that the cinema's most effective 3D films are *Creature from the Black Lagoon* and *House of Wax*, fifties horror films both, and both made using a two camera two projectors set-up. I've only seen those *stereo* films in *mono* 3D bluray which is so consistently effective that once seen one can't ever be satisfied by seeing the 2D version. The original 35mm 3D presentations must have been spectacular, yet I doubt they were better than the presentations of *Friday the 13th 3 3D* that I saw four times in St. Helens in 1983. The 3D in the *Friday the 13th 3*, as screened at the St. Helens ABC, on a brand-new silver screen trumpeted in the local press, was so good the audiences shouted out with genuine amazement. Forget the train and Lumière's workers! The 3D really *really* worked. The depth of protrusion from the screen when, during the opening scene, a clothes pole was pushed out into, and held seemingly across the full depth of the auditorium, was so impressive that in my lifetime of watching real film everywhere and anywhere it hasn't really been matched. The closest to it

was seeing *Born to be Wild* (2011) in 70mm 3D Imax in Seattle. On that same trip, I saw a 3-strip Cinerama print of *How The West Was Won*, the pinnacle of motion-photography as film art. It screened in an original Cinerama cinema restored by America's greatest film collector, Paul G. Allen. The following day, at Allen's Pop culture museum, I drank deep in the black waters of pilgrimage by looking upon the actual mask made by Milicent Patrick for the *Creature of the Black Lagoon*.

Revenge of the Creature, 1955 d. Jack Arnold p. Willam Alland

December 1980 advert from London's fabled Scala cinema

That's Carrie Fisher's father starring in the World Premiere presentation of what became a box-office juggernaut.

Two fascinating adverts. The USA ad for the film's premiere puts almost total emphasis on glamour girls and the technical innovations of 3-D and 'phonic sound', and promises a completely unrealistic 3D height and depth. The result was one of the ten highest grossing films in American history.

The German advert also uses the image of a glamorous girl, but here she is more closely menaced by a black-gloved, black-hatted killer, a founding image for the *krimi* genre that flourished forth in Germany the following year with a long-running series of Edgar Wallace thrillers. The German title echoes two pillars of German horror-thriller cinema: *Caligari*, and *Mabuse*.

House of Wax was flatly remade as *Terror in the Wax Museum* (1973) with Elsa Lanchester, Ray Milland and everyone's favourite orangutan, Maurice Evans (see page 100).

Tarantula, 1955 d. Jack Arnold p. William Alland

It Came from Outer Space, 1953 d. Jack Arnold p. William Alland

The Monolith Monsters, 1957 d. John Sherwood p. Howard Christie story Jack Arnold

Tarantula is the centrepiece of a trilogy of desert horror/science fiction films by Jack Arnold (*It Came From Outer Space, The Monolith Monsters*), tales of invasion in eerie open settings, highways down to the vanishing point, strange rock formations that hide the past and which will have some bearing on the immediate future. Arnold's landscapes aren't the dirty dust deserts of the John Ford Westerns, or the polluted deserts that we will go into with Wes Craven, these are inviting places wrapped around small picture book towns of hour-glass ladies, dependable sheriffs, gleaming automobiles, and the chosen homes of sophisticated articulate square-jawed men of science who will lead the fight. This is Norman Rockwell Americana with a twist.

Warner Brothers' 1954 film about giant ants, *Them!* was probably the spur to *Tarantula* but not the source. Arnold and his screenwriter, Robert M. Fresco, were building on their telefilm, *No Food for Thought,* which screened earlier the same year as part of *Science Fiction Theater* - scientists developing a synthetic food. Arnold's documentary short, *The Chicken of Tomorrow* (1948), already had him thinking about industrial/scientific farming methods.

In *Tarantula*, the synthetic food-of-tomorrow is given an atomic binding that when injected into humans causes quick deformity and death (splendid scary make-up of the style that launched a hundred 1980s horror films). When injected into white rats, a guinea pig and, er, a tarantula (not the most obvious or sensible choice for accelerated growth experiments), all it needs is for someone to break the glass of the spider's cage to get the fun show on the road.

The beast grows so big that the ad art is an understatement! In fact, it needs Clint Eastwood himself (close-ups and dialogue in a precursor for the Tom Hardy-*Dunkirk* role) to *Firefox* in with bombs of Napalm. Play the music Francis!

JOHN AGAR
MARA CORDAY
LEO G. CARROLL
UN NOUVEAU FLÉAU
VA-T-IL RAVAGER
LE MONDE ?
TARANTULA!
Universal International

The Man Without a Body, 1957
d. Charles Saunders, W. Lee Wilder   p. Guido Coen

The Woman Eater 1958
d. Charles Saunders, W. Lee Wilder   p. Guido Coen

By its very nature, Science has always gone beyond the bounds of what is understandable and therefore acceptable to the public at large, and to the authorities in charge. Remember Galileo! Virtually assassinated by the Catholic Church for the crime of looking through a telescope and seeing previously unknown heavenly bodies. Shelley's *Frankenstein* was written partly out of her fears of her husband's experiments with the new fangled discovery of electricity.

The scientist as villain, and scientific experiments as horrific entertainment, came to a renewed fore under the nuclear shadow of the 1950s. The atom bombs of the previous decade meant that, for the first time in human history, Man had the power to destroy the entire world. That fact in itself meant that Science, and therefore men and women of Science, can't be trusted.

The other most untrustable thing to the average filmgoer was Communism. The popular American interpretation of Communism is a crushing reduction of personal and business freedoms, and a penchant for invading other countries. The headless body on the advert for this London-made film is meant to be the reanimated head of Nostradamus but it is modelled on the then brand-new headless body of Karl Marx atop his London tomb, a fact that would be widely known to the public at the time. That alone makes this a rare Reds Under The Beds chiller from the UK. By playing up the psychological dual threat of Mad Scientists and Communism the advert is offering the punter twice the bang for their buck.

On this advert, *Man* is double-billed with the same team's *Woman*. A reviving-the-dead London scientist has a basement full of beakers and a flesh-eating plant. The excellent Edwin Astley title track is scored for cymbals, drums and wordless woman wailing. It's of a professional standard that the rest of the film doesn't reach.

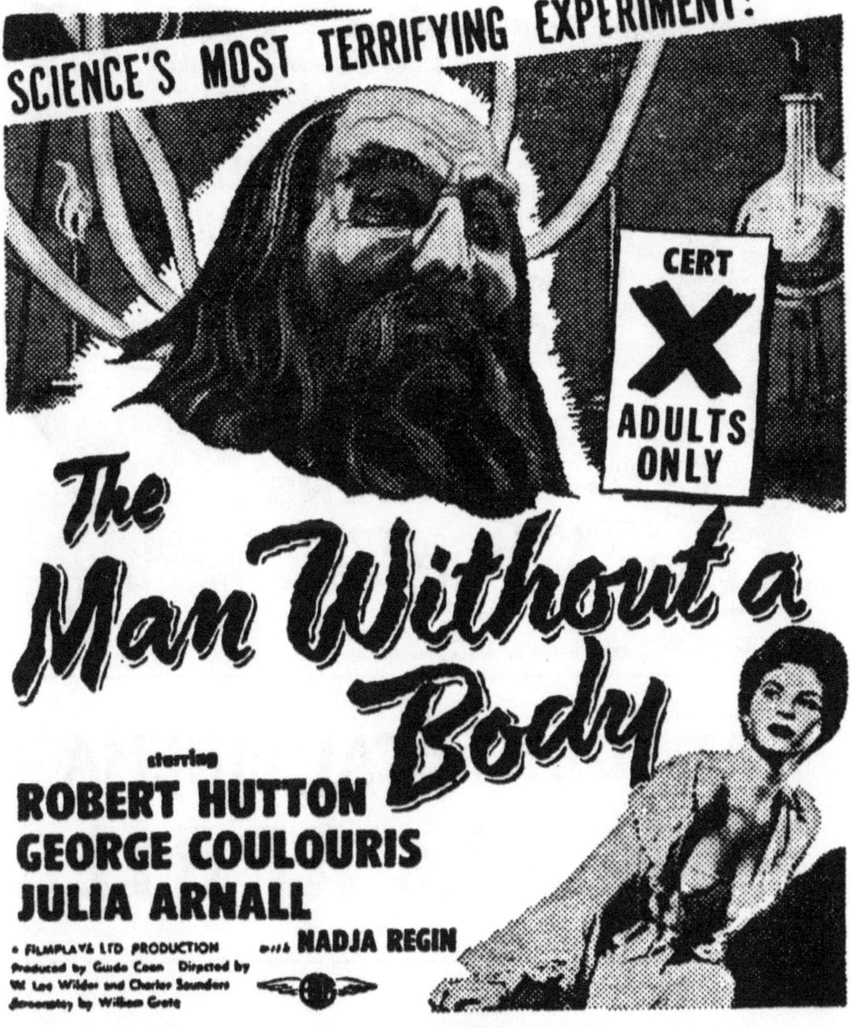

SCIENCE'S MOST TERRIFYING EXPERIMENT!

CERT
X
ADULTS
ONLY

The Man Without a Body

starring
ROBERT HUTTON
GEORGE COULOURIS
JULIA ARNALL

with NADJA REGIN

a FILMPLAYS LTD PRODUCTION
Produced by Guido Coen   Directed by
W. Lee Wilder and Charles Saunders
Screenplay by William Grote

PLUS

SEE
the nerve-shattering
Dance of Death!
SEE
the Woman Eater
ensnare the beauties
of two continents!
SEE
its hideous arms
devour them in a
death-embrace!

GEORGE COULOURIS · VERA DAY
The Woman Eater

Written by BRANDON FLEMING · Produced by GUIDO COEN
Directed by CHARLES SAUNDERS · A FORTRESS FILM PRODUCTION
A COLUMBIA PICTURES RELEASE

1984, 1956 d. Michael Anderson p. N. Peter Rathvon

'*Tense! Terrifying! Terrific!*' and as Orwell's predictions of an all-seeing all-controlling State come largely to be, we can add '*True!*'. I haven't yet seen the Michael Redgrave version but that is a good horrific advert with a strong hint of torture porn. I *have* seen the memorably bleak 1984 adaptation starring a death's door Richard Burton and an emaciated John Hurt. I met the director, Michael Radford, in the green room at the British Film Institute, at a conference on Music and Film, and was nearly assaulted by him when I told him I very much liked the music in his film of *1984*, before back-peddling furiously as his shackles rose and I remembered that those *Sex Crime* Eurythmics songs were imposed on the film by the producers, Virgin Records.

It! The Terror from Beyond Space, 1958
d. Edward L. Cahn, p. Robert E. Kent

Curse of the Faceless Man, 1958
d. Edward L. Cahn, p. Robert E. Kent

I Married a Monster from Outer Space, 1958 d/p Gene Fowler Jr

A shadowy alien with big angry eyes and proto-Krueger hands. In the film, the rather more solid (rubbery) aliens are given a proto-*Altered States* transformation glow accompanied by a dark whirling mists and electronic noise. Great stuff! It's a tale of a doppelgangers and invasion, *Invasion of the Body Snatchers*-lite, but with a flat and wordy script and a teddy boy cast who can't act.

The Blob, 1958 d. Irvin Yeaworth p. Jack H. Harris

With the post-war economies of the West being rebuilt by a new consumerism (selling people things they didn't know they wanted) images of consumption became a growing standard in the Horror film, a subtext often twinned and tripled with the fear of invasion, invasion of the country and invasion of the human body (sexual or by disease). But *The Blob* is just a bit of dumb fun, an independent long-night-of-horror film made in small-town Pennsylvania by a collective of Church and Boy Scout leaders. It is attractively photographed in E.C. comic colours, with a strong understanding of three-dimensional space. The special effects are inventive and successful.

"BLOB" DEVOURS L.A. BOX-OFFICES!
THE BLOB Insatiable... indestructible... indescribable!
THE BLOB
blood-bloated mass of man-eating slime!
THE BLOB in blood-curdling COLOR!
First 5 Days in 36 Pre-release engagements... BIGGEST IN YEARS!
Starring STEVEN McQUEEN
and Co-Starring ANETA CORSEAUT · EARL ROWE
Produced by JACK H. HARRIS
Directed by IRVIN S. YEAWORTH, Jr.
Screenplay by THEODORE SIMONSON and KATE PHILLIPS
From an Idea by IRVINE H. MILLGATE · A TONYLYN Production · Color by DeLUXE
GET READY NOW FOR THIS SLEEPER OF A CREEPER—FROM PARAMOUNT!

THE DIRECTORS OF
HAMMER FILM PRODUCTIONS
MICHAEL CARRERAS
ANTHONY HINDS
JIM CARRERAS
Congratulate
WARNER BROS
ON THEIR

SHOWMANSHIP PLUS!

THIS IS THE ACTUAL ADVERTISEMENT FROM THE
LOS ANGELES EXAMINER
and part of the Terrific Nation-wide press coverage Resulting in *SMASH BUSINESS* all over America.

"THE CURSE OF FRANKENSTEIN"

Directed by **TERENCE FISHER**

The Curse of Frankenstein, 1957 d. Terence Fisher p. Anthony Hinds

Voodoo Island, 1957 d. Reginald Le Borg, p. Howard W. Koch

Koch became head of production at Paramount and produced *Airplane!* and *Ghost.* Of his time with Karloff, filming *Voodoo* Island on the isle of Kauai in Hawaii, he told Tom Weaver (the heavyweight champion of horror film scholarship): "I was in awe of him... It was fun, it was challenging as hell. And I guarantee you, those cheap pictures will stand up against any two-hour movie made today. There's more care and thought in 'em; even though they were low budget, we really *cared* what we were making. We really *tried.*" *Fangoria 46*

And the Horror Film took a giant step forward by bringing in a dark and dangerous eroticism. To the role of Count Dracula, Christopher Lee's genuinely aristocratic presence combines with an athlete's posture that conveys a superhuman strength. It's film acting of the highest order, for Lee acts with his whole body and soul and not just with the words and the mark, a point he was wont to make in the Countless and almost wordless sequels. Here he is being interviewed by Robin Bean on the set of *Dracula Prince of Darkness*: "Dracula is first and foremost a nobleman, a man of great dignity. You notice I emphasise the word *man*; a man of great power, presence, physical impact. A man of broody stillness. When he is in action the demon that is within him, the undead demon which is always clawing to get to the surface, explodes into the most tigerish ferocity and tremendously quick movement. I see him as an abhuman entity who is controlled by a force that is beyond his own powers of control. After all, according to the story in the book he was a great leader, a great general, a great person in every way. And I try, within the limitations of the script and the story that we have, to emphasise the power, not just the physical but the effect of the man's mental capacity." *Films and Filming*, Aug. 1965

Dracula, 1958 d. Terence Fisher p. Anthony Hinds

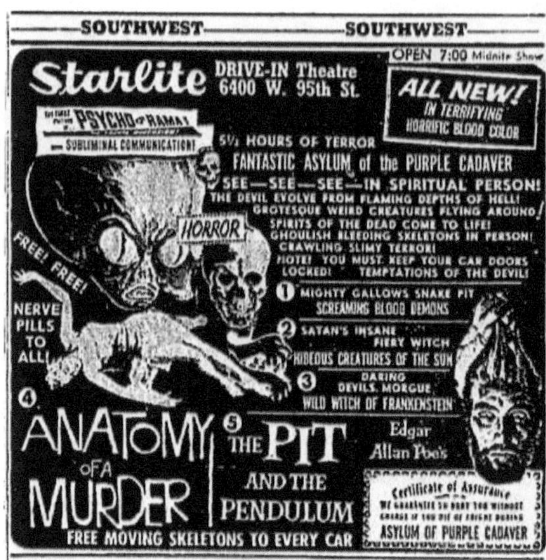

Monster on the Campus, 1958
d. Jack Arnold p. Joseph Gershenson

The Thing That Couldn't Die, 1958
d/p. Will Cowan

Two films written by David Duncan, best known for his fabulous script for *The Time Machine* (1960). Duncan's *Monster on the Campus* was probably 'researched' by Paddy Chayefsky for *Altered States* (1980).

The ad art for *The Thing That Couldn't Die* was so effective it became a staple for the 60's drive-in, repeatedly used on ads on which *The Thing* wasn't billed.

Toute femme
qui le fixe
des yeux
fait d'elle
une esclave
consentante

WILLIAM REYNOLDS
ANDRA MARTIN

LE
DECAPITE
VIVANT

Universal
International

TEST TUBE TERROR-BEAST AMOK IN COLLEGE LAB!

MONSTER ON THE CAMPUS

STARRING ARTHUR FRANZ · JOANNA MOORE WITH JUDSON PRATT
NANCY WALTERS · TROY DONAHUE AND THE BEAST

The Revenge of Frankenstein, 1958
d. Terence Fisher p. Anthony Hinds

Dr. Stein has two successful practises in Carlsbruck. One for the rich. One for the poor. The poor one is a front for 'limb selection' in the construction of a perfect man (Michael Gwynn looking like a cross between Michael Palin and Peter Falk). On the arms of one of the poor men *is A Tattoo!* These were the days before fan conventions and football. Literate Hammer with a big cast and lots of *acting*, dozens of good professional stage players given a chance to don a costume and roll an eye.

The Leech Woman, 1960
d. Edward Dein p. Joseph Gershenson

A fist-clenched woman about to ring-punch a gun-wielding assistant with painted nails. *The Leech Woman* ad is particularly interesting for the words 'Midi Minuit' (Version Originale) in the upper left corner. Midi Minuit was a fabled cinema on the boulevard Poissonnières in Paris. It opened from noon until midnight, specialised in films that made bluestockings blanche, and inspired France's first literary-pictorial journal dedicated to the genre: *Midi-Minuit Fantastique*.

Horrors of Spider Island, 1960 d. Fritz Böttger p. Wolf C. Hartwig, Gaston Hakim

Horror, 1963 d. Alberto de Martino p. Gianni Grimaldi

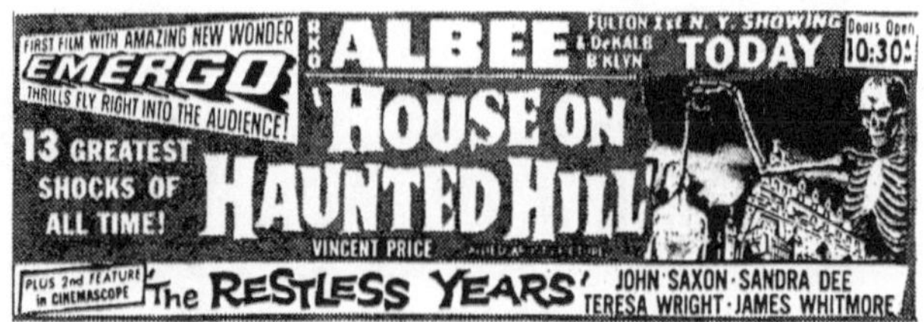

House on Haunted Hill, 1959 d/p. William Castle

As haunted houses go this one is a stunner from the outside, like a modernist Aztec temple as designed by Frank Lloyd Wright. It catches the viewer completely unaware - an original setting. Alas, when the cast move inside, all we get is an overlit sound-stage dressed in *faux* Gothic with cobwebs and chandeliers. Pity. Then comes long layers of talky exposition. More than half a film of it! Five needy people are to be paid thousands if they stay a night. Where's Linda Blair in a bodice when you need her? Great ad art though.

The Brides of Dracula, 1960
d. Terence Fisher   p. Anthony Hinds

In a very real way, the Hammer films are a sort of late 20th Century Grimm. A generation of children saw their first Hammer Horrors on late night TV, a regular attraction, food for our fears, art that grew our imagination. They became a part of who we are. We are the children of Hammer.

The City of the Dead, 1960
d. John Llewellyn Moxey
p. Max Rosenberg, Don Taylor

The American adverts from 1963 grab our attention and tells us to expect a buxom blonde checking into a hotel next to a graveyard where she'll be attacked by fanged zombies (a sort of fever dream prophecy for *Night of the Living Dead*). What they don't tell us is to expect a quietly impressive chiller, atmospherically photographed in black-and-white; a film that serves up a real sense of growing dread and which features Christopher Lee lecturing on the occult. Yes, it's almost a dry run for *The Wicker Man*!

Patricia Jessel impresses as the best Danvers-style housekeeper outside of *Rebecca*. Her performance here is worth the price of admission. She had just made a film with a tiny blond boy with round staring eyes...

Village of the Damned, 1960
d. Wolf Rilla p. Ronald Kinnoch

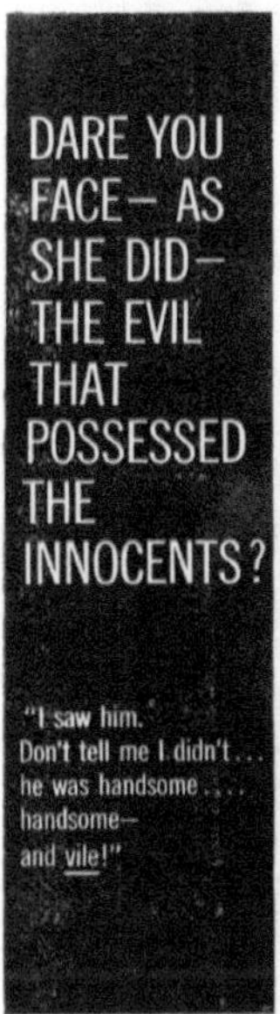

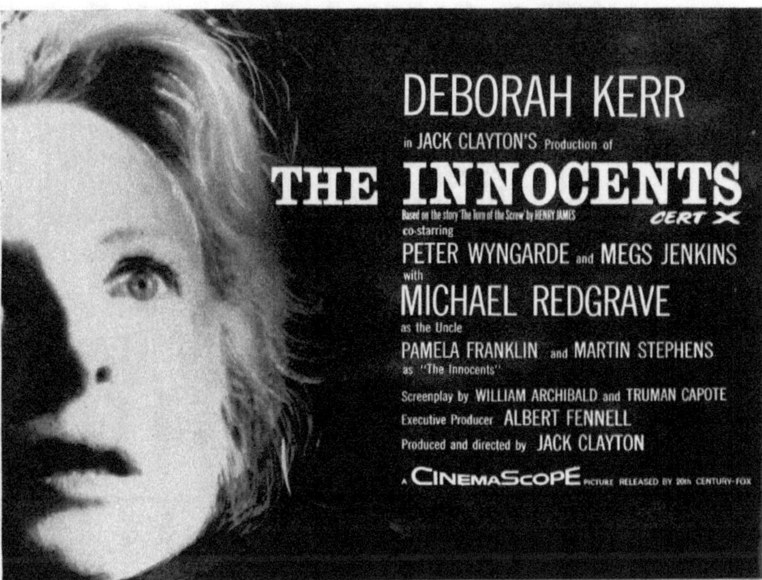

The Innocents, 1961
d/p. Jack Clayton

After appearing with Patricia Jessel in *No Kidding*, where he played a sad and lonely Scottish boy at Leslie Phillip's summer school (not a good film), ten-year-old Martin Stephens prepared to meet Henry James's Miss Jessel by first being wigged blonder than Mansfield to gang-lead a scary group of seminal invaders in *Village of the Damned*. A miraculously effective film if one saw the German director's previous Invading England effort, *Bachelor of Hearts*. Filmed in Eastmancolor on location at Cambridge University, *Bachelor* starred a real-life über-Aryan (and Hitler Youth graduate) Hardy Kruger. In one scene, Kruger is 'human sacrificed' by English twits in a red-robed rag-stunt. Barbara Steele cameos! Though repeatedly dragged down by a rotten script (by Leslie Bricusse AND Frederic Raphael!), *Bachelor of Hearts* is styleless and directionless, which tells me that *Village of the Damned* was a fluke. An accidentally brilliant B-Movie.

After scaring the world in *Village of the Damned*, Martin Stephens gave an even better scary-child performance in an even better film, *The Innocents*, a genuine A-lister. Kerr (who first acted with Stephens in *Count Your Blessings*) sees horrors, or are they just projections of a repressed and dirty mind? Her stay at the children's mansion starts with the cry of a hurt animal and ends with the screams of a boy. Truman Capote himself wrote the dialogue and deservedly took pride in his achievement. Peerless black-and-white cinemascope photography by double Oscar Winner, Freddie Francis, whose work was never better than it is here.

Psycho, 1960 d/p. Alfred Hitchcock

What can be said about *Psycho* that hasn't already been said or published? Nothing probably. The film deserves all the admiration and praise. It is peerless thriller cinema. Revisiting it last year after buying the bluray, I grinned from ear to ear with pleasure whilst watching it again and listening to the new restoration of the soundtrack. With great subtlety and intelligence, the sound mix has been tweaked to make it immersive. We almost feel the all-enveloping rain. Hitchcock would be thrilled. I say that with whole-hearted respect, and as a man who stands firmly on the side of The People in the vs George Lucas .

Peeping Tom, 1960 d/p. Michael Powell

La Casa del Terror (House of Terror), 1959
d. Gilberto Martínez Solares p/sc. Fernando de Fuentes

Splendid German advert for the Mexican science-lab wax-museum horror film made to cash-in on the Abbott and Costello monster movies and starring the self-same Hollywood werewolf. Chaney, hairier and wilder than in his Universal days, goes night prowling up and over a skyscraper in present day Mexico City. Tin-Tan has the Lou Costello role. The stealing of Tin-Tan's blood gets the show started.

You can count the good horror films about boys on the fingers of one hand, but schoolgirls? Schoolgirls! What heights and depths the horror film would be missing if it had to make do without them! From the sublime Technicolor English roses of the English *Brides of Dracula*, and the lovely young American lost in Italo-Germany's *Suspiria*, down to new age thrills like *Schoolgirl Apocalypse* (2011). Loitering at the lower to mid-level of this favourite sub-genre is the dead black-and-white of *Lychanthropus*, a skin-free Austrian prototype of the women in prison genre where every inmate is gorgeous. Atmospheric exteriors in a very real castle surrounded by howling wolves and middle-age men, but it's a slow tale of blackmail and murder and something daft to do with the dogs. A marketing maestro at MGM gave it the Got-My-Interest title and added a wholly inappropriate but fun perk-it-up surf song, *The Ghoul in School*.

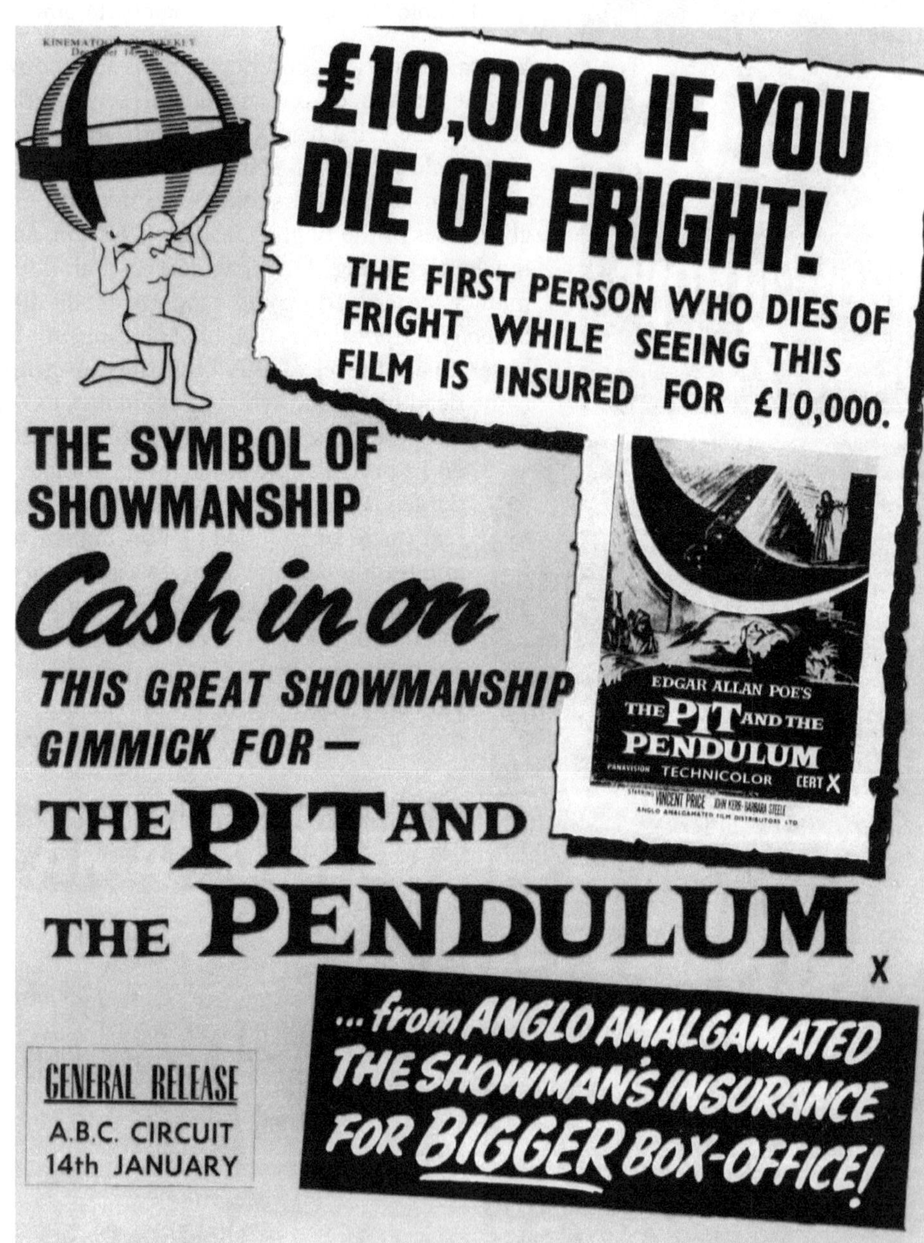

The Pit and the Pendulum, 1961
d/p. Roger Corman
exec-p, James H. Nicholson

The Curse of the Werewolf, 1961
d. Terence Fisher p. Anthony Hinds

Oliver Reed, the darkest and most dangerous English actor of his generation, was the perfect werewolf but this is not the definitive werewolf film. It doesn't overcome the flaws in its construction. The first half is wolf-less, and Reed's is not a strongly directed performance (he did need a strong director). Perversely, for what I'm about to say goes against all critical fashion, I much prefer *The Wolfman,* not the beloved Lon Chaney Jr. classic, but the much-maligned reboot made in 2010 by Joe Johnston and starring the-best-Reed-lookalike, Benicio Del Toro. It is everything the Fisher-Hinds-Reed film fails to be: gory atmospheric fun with scares and spectacle aplenty. Then again, I did see *The Wolfman* on its opening night at the Electric Cinema in Birmingham and I've only seen the Hammer film on TV.

Black Sunday, 1960 d. Mario Bava p. Massimo De Rita

The Hour When Dracula Comes. But what they meant was it's the hour-and-half that made Barbara Steele a horror icon, though it did take decades for Steele's appeal to spread from the heartlands of Continental Europe to the UK and the United States. The main reasons for the delay was the strange fact the film was banned outright in the UK until 1968 and then poorly distributed. In the States it was AIP-ed (i.e. re-edited) onto Roger Corman double-bills. We didn't know what we were missing.

The Girl Who Knew Too Much, 1963
d. Mario Bava p. Massimo De Rita

An American girl assaulted in Rome witnesses an ABC murder. The plot line on which the multi-national *giallo* was built. *Girl* is from a time when smoking on aeroplanes was encouraged and full-length snakeskin coats had bite. The whole film is framed with an elaborate marijuana gag as if to establish this as the first *rock-and-roll giallo*. It's certainly the last and most modern of the black-and-white Bava's. A busy narrator, taken in style from the French New Wave, lets us in on the protagonist's thoughts, often at Rome's top tourist spots, and gets in the way of the consistently inventive staging. The first two death scenes are stunning. I do like the scratching of the cat.

The Fall of the House of Usher, 1961 d/p. Roger Corman

Vincent Price's Usher wears a long red dress coat with a white lace shirt dressing. His rooms are curtained with long red drapes and a white lace lining. He and the House are one and the same, cut from the same cloth, if you pardon the pun. We are invited to watch both of them fall, though *invited* is perhaps not the right word for this fine film about a resolutely reclusive man. The booming voice of his sister's suitor (Mark Damon) hurts his ears, his cultivated tastes and his damaged mind. Each sparking wince of Frederick Usher stores power for the building flames. It's a fascinating wholly enjoyable star performance. Of course the Academy Award that year went to Gregory Peck in a Good Man role (stealing it from the rightful mantelpiece of Peter O'Toole, whose richly dark and damaged Lawrence of Arabia was the year's other true landmark in screen acting).

Curiously, Mark Damon's wooden out-of-his-depth performance *was* garlanded by the Golden Globes. Given the Best Newcomer prize, he was scouted off to Italy by the real-life castle-living sensitive Count of Lonate Pozzolo, known to you and me as the great Luchino Visconti, a connoisseur of male beauty. But where Vincent Price's Usher takes the American horror film into the modern age, Damon's black-and-white approach, and brillcreamed Teddy Boy locks, keep pulling it back to the 1950s. Craft and intelligence do win out in the end because of Price's artistry and because the script doesn't play down to the audience. For example, it's taken as a given that we know what is meant, and how it applies to the plot, when the loyal butler listing the family's woes, accidentally says, "Narc...".

Corman's ready use of a thrilling ferocious bass rumble as the sound of the disturbed house means the film is ripe for a Sensurround upgrade.

Santo contra los zombies, 1961 d. Benito Alazraki p. Alberto López

La invasión de los vampiros, 1963 d. Miguel Morayta p. Rafael Pérez Grovas

Nightmare, 1964 d. Freddie Francis p. Jimmy Sangster

El mundo de los vampiros, 1961 d. Alfonso Corona Blake p. Abel Salazar

Mondo Cane 2, 1963 d. Gualtiero Jacopetti, Franco Prosperi

The Mondo films, or films of true-life horrors and unpleasant sights, were born from the most innocent and uplifting films: the Cinerama travelogues, with their beautiful people visiting lovely places. It wasn't so much the cine-grandeur of Cinerama that appealed to such darkside-tourists-as-director as Prosperi, but rather their massive profits. *This is Cinerama* was the biggest money-making film in the world in 1952 AND 1953. Move aside the choristers and water skiers, cage the dogs and slaughter the pigs.

Hercules in the Haunted World, 1961 d. Mario Bava p. Achille Piazzi

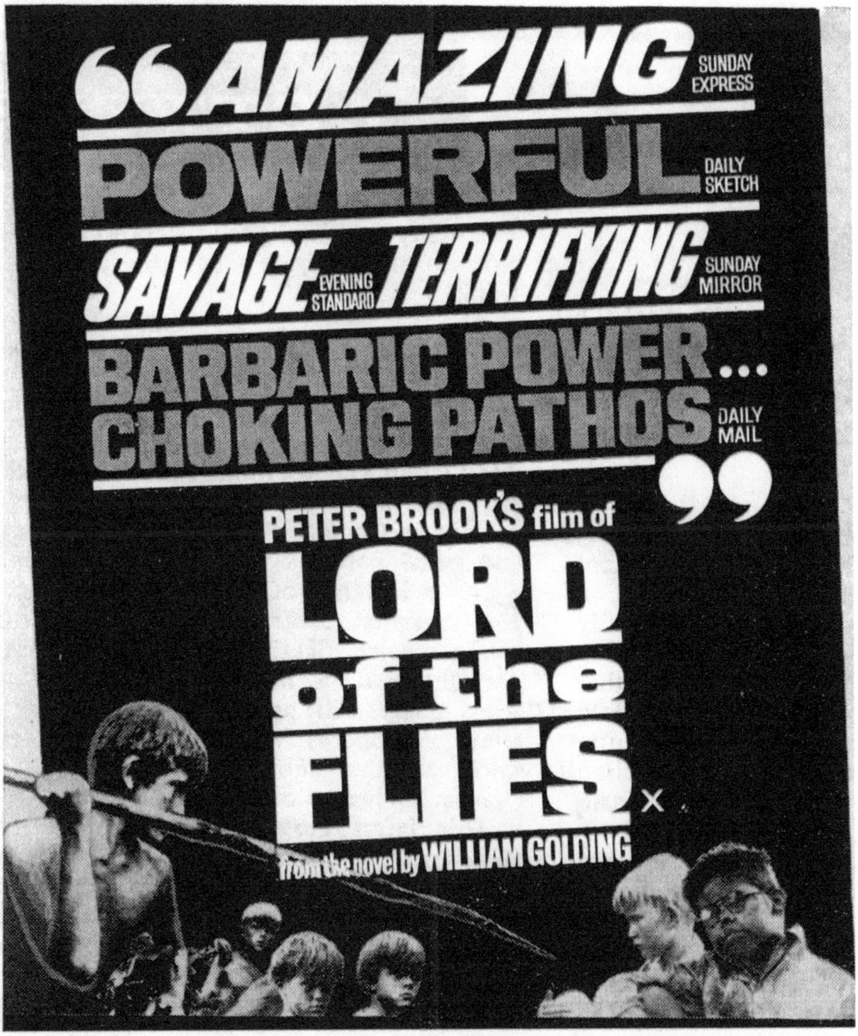

Lord of the Flies, 1963
d. Peter Brook p. Lewis M. Allen

A parachutist lands on a lovely desert island but finding it populated by forty public schoolboys kills himself immediately, and haunts them through the head of a pig.

Carnival of Souls, 1963
d/p Herk Hervey

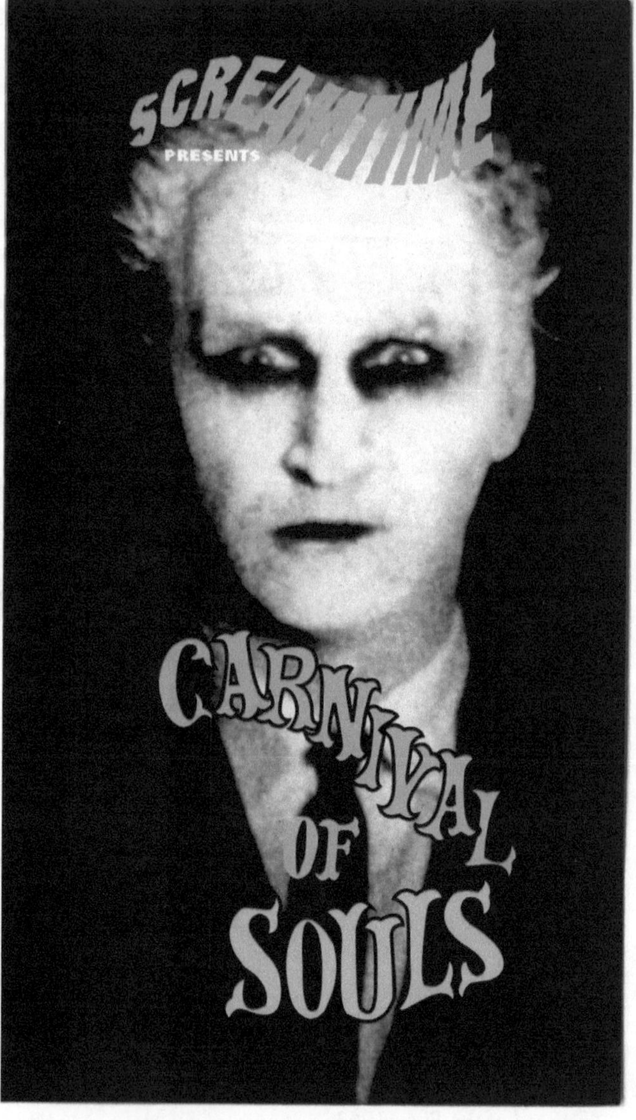

Are there any no-budgeters as effective on a first viewing as this? With its great air of sadness and strangeness, and those camera and sound tricks that seem to have inspired David Lynch's *Grandmother*? And David too probably.

Never having seen a good print in the cinema, only copies on TV and on VHS, I became privy to the film's success when I saw the version that Criterion restored and released on blu-ray. I always knew the film had *something*, but now I know what that something is. It's Maurice Prather - the cinematographer. He's an undiscovered genius. His work is as good as anything you'll see in a Fellini film, given Prather's limitations. He has no understanding of studio lighting, and it shows in the one scene in the film shot in a studio, but out on the streets and in true-life locations, like the skeleton of that gorgeous pier ballroom, he's as good as you'll see. I understand that Prather preferred still photography to making films. He died leaving only this feature film, some documentary work (also with Herk Hervey), and a lot of stills and negatives. Please Maurice Prather's family, get a publisher for Maurice's photographs, and let us enjoy and celebrate an American master.

The only director to get his picture on the ads. The gala advert on the right was published in the *Detroit Free Press*, 30 May '63.

The Birds, 1963
d/p. Alfred Hitchcock

The film's horror set-pieces are so effective, and directed with such élan and humour that studies of the film tend to reduce the film thus. But I think the most impressive things about *The Birds* are the writing, the characterisations, the way Hitchcock introduces each character. Particularly impressive is the first scene between Hepburn and Pleschette. A Hitchcock blonde and a Hitchcock brunette. Whole histories rise in the spaces between the words. It goes beyond Bergmanesque. It's filmmaking of the highest order.

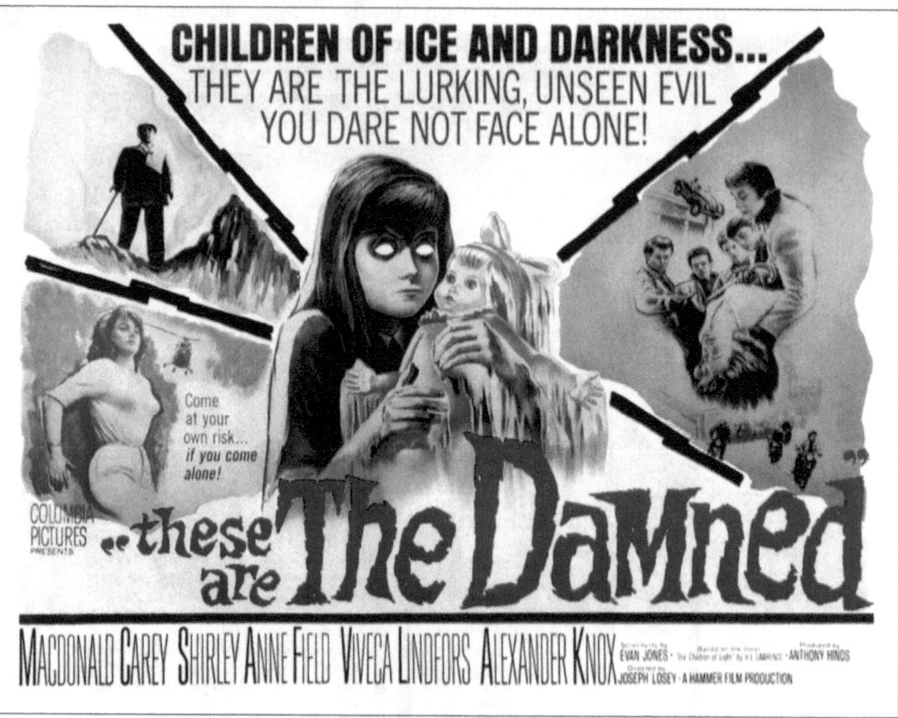

The Damned, (made in 1961, released in 1963)
d. Joseph Losey p. Michael Carreras, Anthony Hinds

Forced out of his own country by an endemically corrupt FBI empowered by a weak government, American Joseph Losey found sanctuary in the freedoms of England and Europe where he made a long run of fine films about abuses of Establishment Power, from *The Damned* and *Accident* to *The Assassination of Trotsky* and *Les Routes du Sud.*

The Damned is a schizophrenic but effective film that could be read as a potted history of American power from Puritan bullies (the sex-obsessed but virginal brother and sister played by Oliver Reed and Shirley Anne Field) through to the annihilation-minded madmen in control of nuclear weapons. Caught in the crossfire are a middle-aged American on holiday (representing Losey himself?); a European artist whose statuary represents the destruction of great civilisations (from Ancient Greece to Roman Pompeii and Hiroshima) and nine articulate and loving English children named after monarchs. The children are said to be the offspring of people killed in atomic accidents, an explanation that rings hollow coming as it does from the lips of a government stooge, nicely characterised with shades of grey, who is ever ready to put State policy ahead of human decency.

Paranoiac, 1963   d. Freddie Francis p. Anthony Hinds

There are pistols on the mantelpiece and swords on the walls, so you know it's not going to be a film of happy families, though it is a tale of brotherly love. It's the second Hammer coastal jolly of 1963 starring Oliver Reed. *The Damned's* sea views were dressed by Elizabeth Frink's burnt body statues. There are no such riches of detail here. It's a film of mostly Bray interiors and gardens with the sea views being used for crude blue-screen backdrops. But *Paranoiac* does have a memorable contribution by a female artist: a full orchestral score by Elisabeth Lutyens, full of straining Schönberg strings and mournful horns, and it does have an attractive impassioned performance by Janette Scott. Reed watchers will note that the film opens with a very mobile camera going round a tomb and taking in an impressive post-funeral oration, very much like in Oliver's masterpiece, *The Devils.* Though Ken Russell told me the only Reed-Hammer film he ever saw was "The werewolf one." Reed here is all slouching, swaggering, grinning, shouting, whispering and boozing. Unless you're very strong in the cups, it is not a good film to watch as a drinking game.

The horror film as a carnival sideshow. Beauties and blood. *Blood Feast* earned its place in film history by serving up MORE than it promised (well, if we discount the expectations raised by that *Playboy* tag line). Though broadly adolescent, Lewis's films were still too advanced for the British distributors and censors so they didn't play in theatres here, and were quite inaccessible until the home video age. But in the dark days of censorship, an uncut 35mm print of *Two Thousand Maniacs!* was smuggled into the country, I think by everyone's favourite crazy uncle, Lloyd Kaufman, and given a single screening at London's National Film Theatre (on a double-bill with *Rabid Grannies*). I was not a member, all the tickets had been sold and I was living in Liverpool at the time. But I still got in.

Blood Feast, 1963
d/p. Herschell Gordon Lewis

Two Thoussand Maniacs!, 1964 d. H. G. Lewis p. David F. Friedman

The advert conveys a thrilling graveyard gothic atmosphere that the film does not have. It's a brightly coloured daytime tale of laughing hick town torturers and slaughters rolling out the barrel. Citizens of a Southern town wiped out by Yankees get revenge every hundred years when the ghosts of the dead lure Northerners to the Centennial celebrations.

The Evil of Frankenstein, 1964 d. Freddie Francis p. Anthony Hinds

The Kiss of the Vampire, 1963
d. Don Sharp   p. Anthony Hinds

Hammer, Amicus and Hallam
(Harry Alan Towers) combine
on a triple-bill in Los Angeles.

King Kong vs Godzilla, 1962 d. Ishirō Honda p. Tomoyuki Tanaka

British press advert for the X-rated film BANNED to the under sixteens (above). Oh, the silly prattery of censors. In July 1970 the age restriction for X certificate films was raised to eighteen.

King Kong Escapes, 1967
d. Ishirō Honda p. Tomoyuki Tanaka

1974 American advert proving that genre films can run and run at the box-office. Good to see Kong twinned with an Abbott and Costello, whose Universal Monster Mashes didn't get round to it.

The Horrible Dr. Hichcock, 1963
d. Riccardo Freda p. Luigi Carpentieri, Ermanno Donati

An influential Italian horror film of English manners, candles, hypodermic needles, a black cat, and a gentleman's kink in the locked room (off screen). It starts with a ferocious all-drums-a-blazing soundtrack, for a few bars, an approach to horror film scoring that caught Dario Argento's attention, to say nothing of the use of bold red or yellow lighting at moments of suspense and danger. But this is not an exciting film. Not a lot happens. A full twenty minutes pass before Barbara Steele arrives looking divine. Roman Vlad fiddles in Rome but in a style that suggests he is auditioning for Dick Barton. All burns down of course.

"THE CURSE of the MUMMY'S TOMB"

The Curse of the Mummy's Tomb, 1963 d/p/sc. Michael Carreras

For a few years in the early 1960s, British distributors who made the press campaign books, offered comic strips, alongside the usual posters and lobby cards, designed to run for four or five days in local newspapers. Unlike admats, the strips were loaned for free, but cinema owners still had to pay for the newspaper space. The take up wasn't good. Made at Elstree instead of Bray and benefitting from spacious settings, *Mummy's Tomb* has bright widescreen (Techniscope) photography and literate if unimaginative writing. The only real downsides are the lack of star power and horror. Burmese actress, Jeanne Roland is dull-dubbed into a monotone French-accented English and, inexplicably, gets all the long speeches and the exposition! Thus is rendered flat every scene she is in. Fred Clark brings a pleasant energy as the American paymaster and showman who gets his own way. A metaphor for Hammer's relationship with the States?

The Horror of Party Beach, 1964, *The Curse of the Lving Corpse*, 1964
d/p. Del Tenney

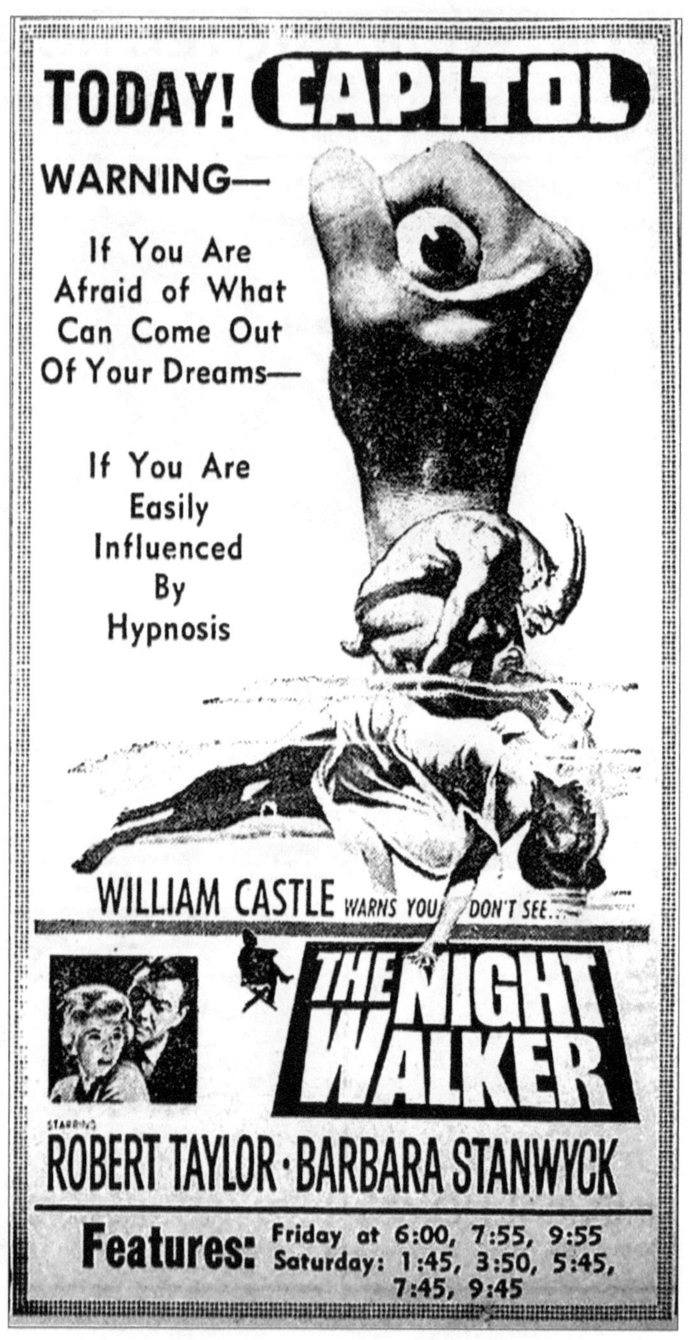

The Night Walker, 1964 d/p. William Castle

A fabulous demon-and-maiden image inspired by Henry Fuseli's painting, *The Nightmare*. Paul Dufficey would use the same famous Fuseli for the poster art for Ken Russell's *Gothic* (1987).

The Haunting, 1963
d/p Robert Wise

Strait-Jacket, 1963
d/p. William Castle

Trog, 1970
d .Freddie Francis, Herman Cohen

I was a teenage friend of Guerrilla filmmaker, Chris Jones. Chris had an 8mm 'shadows and falling heads' highlight reel of *Strait-Jacket*. It was fun. Though still a child I was already a film scholar. I struggled to equate Joan Crawford's high reputation with *The Gorgeous Hussy*'s performance here. I hadn't seen *Baby Jane*, of course... or *Trog*...

The Fool Killer, 1965
d. Servando González p. David Friedkin

An atmospheric slice of Southern Gothic with a child performance of such haunting pain and power that the film resonates long after it is over. An orphaned boy runs away from cruel foster parents and finds only madness in the post-Civil-War States. A thrilling work of real cinema with Perkins broadening the dangerous loner role he perfected in *Psycho* (1960), which this advert references in the tag-line about latecomers not being admitted.

Black Sabbath, 1963 d. Mario Bava p. Alberto Barsanti, Samuel Z. Arkoff

The Collector, 1965 d. William Wyler p. Jud Kinberg, John Kohn

Leaving behind big *Ben-Hur* and the cleaning air of *The Big Country*, William Wyler cast a fresh eye on London and the English countryside and locked himself away in an old dark room. His achievements here are mighty. The city has rarely been photographed more vividly than it is in the opening scenes of this impressive disquieting horror film. The full-focus on-the-move photography is so immersive and true it's a pity the film has to move inside to the keeper's lair. Terence Stamp has the Norman Bates role. Samantha Eggar is the victim. They're both tragically human, particularly Eggar. Hers is the character that evolves, hers the emotions that climb and fall. It's one of the genre's great performances. Those wanting to trace the genesis of *The Silence of the Lambs* will find the markers here, from the butterflies to the stillness of the beast, the entrapment vehicle, the secluded basement, the social inferiority that stings.

The Torture Chamber of Dr. Sadism, 1967
d. Harald Reinl p. Erwin Gitt

Karin Dor in two good slices of full German gothic made by her husband, Harald Reinl.

The Strangler of Blackmoor Castle, 1963 d. Harald Reinl p. Artur Brauner

The Mad Executioners, 1963 d. Edwin Zbonek p. Artur Brauners

England, and London especially, was the go-to place for the German horror film, not because of a nationalistic fear but because the German public adored (and adore) the dark and methodical violent novels of Edgar Wallace.

The Undertaker and His Pals, 1966 d T. Swicegood p. Alex Grattan

There's more professional artistry on the ad than there is in this cheap film of red-paint gore, green painted sets and white and black brassieres, played mostly to a grating improvised sax score. *The Undertaker* is pitched between TVs *Batman* and what will become *The Texas Chainsaw Massacre*, for which it offers up a few scenes of inspiration - bodies on meathooks, the highway chase of a woman ending with the assailant's collision with a truck. A gang of whackos sell human meat in part to boost takings for one of life's most insidious true-life scams - the undertaker business. The Shady Rest undertaker (Ray Dannis) has a hint of the Pee-wee Herman about him and even does a one-legged skateboard ride. It's not as much fun as it sounds.

The Boston Strangler, 1968 d. Richard Fleischer p. James Cresson, Robert Fryer

Richard Fleischer made great films in more genres than any man. From the Disney wonderlands of *20,000 Leagues Under the Sea* to the nihilist future of *Soylent Green,* the eye-plucking history of *The Vikings* and the courtroom thriller of *Compulsion,* the all-singing Neil Diamond *Jazz Singer* and Charles Bronson getting melon-smashing mad in *Mr. Majestyk,* to name only the first that come into my head. Actually, my favourite film by Fleischer is *Doctor Doolittle,* the Rex Harrison version. I like its air of refined English eccentricity and Samantha Eggar in boots. I saw it in 70mm with an audience of eight old crew members and one hundred and fifty attentive children rustling fifty-thousand wrappers of sweets. "Will somebody *please* get me a shotgun!"

American madness though is the theme of *The Boston Strangler.* Mass murdering nutters do turn up all over the world but the modern serial killer is very much an American phenomenon. I suppose it's because the country spent its adolescence over-admiring gun-tooting villains in the wilds of the West. They always put the villain on Page One.

Fleischer's *The Boston Strangler,* an outstanding work of film art, was probably the first Establishment horror film. The emphasis is not on the killings, which are not shown, nor on the victims, who are thinly sketched. The film is about the thoroughness of the Establishment investigation, the police, the doctors, the near pure perfect District Attorney man (Henry Fonda, of course), who brings the strands of the investigation together and gets the man - after taking us through a colourful parade of deviants. The deviation route is used perhaps to educate the wider public, but really to make Nutter Number One seem normal. A genuine frisson is felt when the quiet reveal is made and we see The Boston Strangler with his wife and young children.

A solemn appeal is made not to destroy such mentally damaged men but to study them. The Strangler here is said to have a split personality, one half innocent of what the other half is doing. It's Jekyll and Hyde but with added shrink consultation fees. This split personality is represented in the first four-fifths of the film by the use of split screen. The same event shown from different angles with emphasis on different details. There are screen-splits of differing shapes and sizes, very much like the pioneering work of Charles and Ray Eames in their multi-screen films for the New York World Fair in 1964. The final section is in a white room cleanly filmed in clear light with long takes so we can enjoy the star actor at his craft.

Twisted Nerve, 1966 d John Boulting p. Roy Boulting

The Boultings were sort of English Coen Brothers. Inseparable siblings working in productive harmony and at their best when making comedy. Peter Sellers was a Boulting graduate. Here they twist the nerves of Hayley Mills, a Disney graduate. Disney kids often rush to the cleanse themselves in the dark side after a long childhood built on a pedestal of smiles. Alas, Hywel Bennett is never convincing.

"Come in."
He did. Thirteen times.
20th Century-Fox presents
THE BOSTON STRANGLER
X
The people and events depicted are based on fact!
STARRING
TONY CURTIS · HENRY FONDA · GEORGE KENNEDY
CO STARRING
Mike Kellin Murray Hamilton
PRODUCED BY   DIRECTED BY   SCREENPLAY BY
Robert Fryer Richard Fleischer Edward Anhalt
BASED ON THE BOOK BY
Gerold Frank   Panavision®
Colour by DeLuxe.
ON RELEASE AT ODEON
AND OTHER LEADING CINEMAS
NORTH LONDON from JUNE 15
SOUTH LONDON from JUNE 22

COMING SOON AT
ABC AND OTHER
LEADING CINEMAS
Enough
to make even
Hitchcock
jump!
YOU ARE INSURED FOR £25,000 IN CASE YOU DIE OF FRIGHT
WHILE SEEING 'TWISTED NERVE'
THE BOULTING BROTHERS'
HAYLEY MILLS   HYWEL BENNETT
TWISTED NERVE
'X'
BILLIE WHITELAW   PHYLLIS CALVERT
BARRY FOSTER   SALMAAN PEER
Guest star FRANK FINLAY
Produced by GEORGE W GEORGE & FRANK GRANAT
Screenplay by LEO MARKS & ROY BOULTING
A BRITISH LION PRESENTATION
EASTMAN COLOUR

Planet of the Apes, 1968 d. Franklin J Schaffner p. Arthur P. Jacobs

A very important advert placed in the *Los Angeles Times*
on the eve of the release of the landmark film.

The Devil Rides Out, 1968
d. Terence Fisher p. Anthony Nelson-Keys

The most inept fight choreography I've ever seen is in Robert Bresson's *Mouchette* (1967), but this film runs it close and it does have a lot of fist fights. Two friends of his father aim to save a rich young man from a black magic cult. One cringes at a plot flaw that allows a group of adults to leave a child alone in bed while they protect themselves from Invading Evil by standing in a protective safe-space ring downstairs (or am I'm projecting present day values on a tale of times past?). This otherwise well-plotted Hammer film overcomes poor continuity (blood-spattered onto a white dress is gone in the next shot; lighting within scenes changes from dark to dusk and from dusk to dark) because it is ram full of entertaining surprises, such as Christopher Lee wrecking a Bacchanalian baptism by driving a vintage motorcar through it! Lee, a friend of Dennis Wheatley who lived on the same square in Chelsea, appointed himself as the film's "black mass technical adviser" and came up with the words for the climactic exorcism.

Tenderness of the Wolves, 1973
d. Ulli Lommel p. Rainer Werner Fassbinder, Michael Fengler

Le Vampire de Dusseldorf, 1965
d. Robert Hossein p. Georges de Beauregard, Benito Perojo

In the early 1970s, a bald head was the very definition of madness (spin the wheel of any Ken Russell film and find yourself an example, or look at the ads for *The Hills Have Eyes*). The very few men with bald heads in the 1970s, such as swimmer Duncan Goodhew and Telly Savalas, made a career out of it. Then along came the skinhead movement, the gay liberation movement, that 'alien' woman in the slow expensive *Star Trek* film, and the bald head was suddenly everywhere. I was watching the rugby on TV three or four years back. The three male presenters, ex-players in their 30s, had all shaved their heads completely as a sign they were fully peer-pressured up into 'owning' their middle-aged baldness. What I'm trying to say is that the London press advert on the left would have shouted out 'Mad Man!' to the public in 1973. The madness denoted by the bald head of Kurt Raab and not the fact his lips are dripping with a man's blood. Present day viewers of *Tenderness* will probably be taken aback by its male nudity which nobody noticed back then. It's a dark sad film about emptiness. *Tenderness of the Wolves* is Düsseldorf 3. I have not seen Düsseldorf 2. Düsseldorf 1 was the mighty Fritz Lang's *M*.

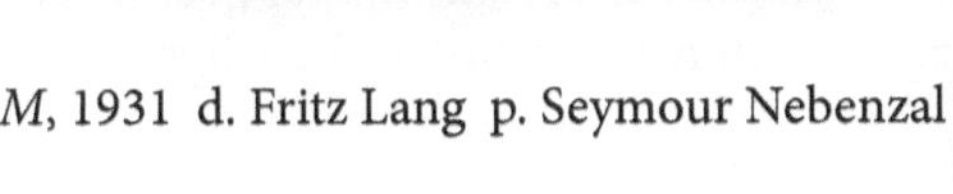

M, 1931 d. Fritz Lang p. Seymour Nebenzal

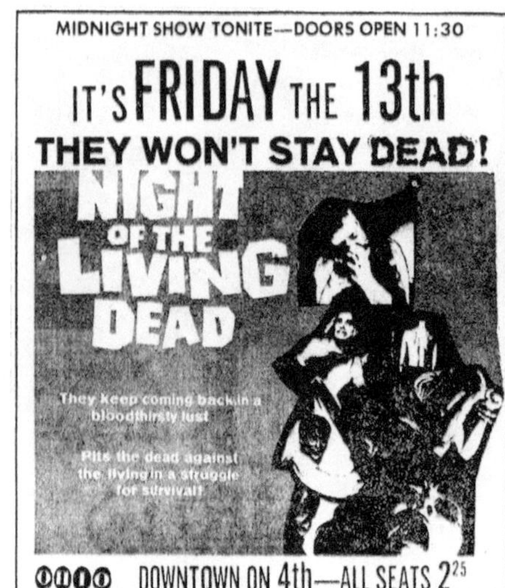

25 years later and still the king of the drive-in.

Night of the Living Dead, 1968 d/p. George A. Romero p. Richard Rubinstein

The strong British advert is sure to bring the punters in, but it's clear that the artist who did it a) hadn't seen the film and b) couldn't visualise what was told to him in his brief. Chances are he was simply working from the title. Without seeing the film how could he know he was illustrating a landmark? a masterpiece? On paper, *Night of the Living Dead* seems to be a B-movie remake of Hitchcock's *The Birds* - a blonde in shock, the boarding up of an isolated farmhouse, the siege by nature gone mad, all scored with electronic sound effects. It's all that and more. Much more.

I attended my first public screening of this Cuban-American Gift to the World when I was 13-years-old. The venue: the Haydock Labour Club No.1, a working man's club with tables and chairs for 500 which specialised in violent double-bills - *Dirty Harry* and *I Spit on Your Grave, Dressed to Kill* and *Cannibal Ferox*. When they wanted to tone it down for a Christmas all-dayer, they'd put on *Animal House,* a *Lemon Popsicle* film, *The Wanderers* and the Neil Diamond version of *The Jazz Singer*. We'd all sing *Sweet Caroline* in gratitude whilst drinking 11-pence half-pints of shandy. Happy days. Being a members' club there were no restrictions and no censorship, although the doorman was known to turn away the under tens if it was an *Exorcist* or a 'video nasty'. "Don't worry love. We're putting that monkey one on with Clint Eastwood next week. You can come and see that." And all the while the politicians and the censors and the news editors were screaming themselves into a More Censorship hysteria as a sideshow distraction to the country's economic ills (the government actively destroying the industrial and manufacturing industries and cities); to turn the public eye away from their own hand-in-the-tillery; and to stop the independents from taking business from the Rank and Hollywood mainstream. There has always been less crime and more common sense in Haydock than in Westminster.

All of that true-life-in-the-early-eighties ramble is to say that of all the horror films projected onto the big video screen at Haydock Labour Club No.1, and there was many, *The Night of the Living Dead* went down the best. A full club of beered-up men, women and children nodding quiet appreciation as the end of show lights went up.

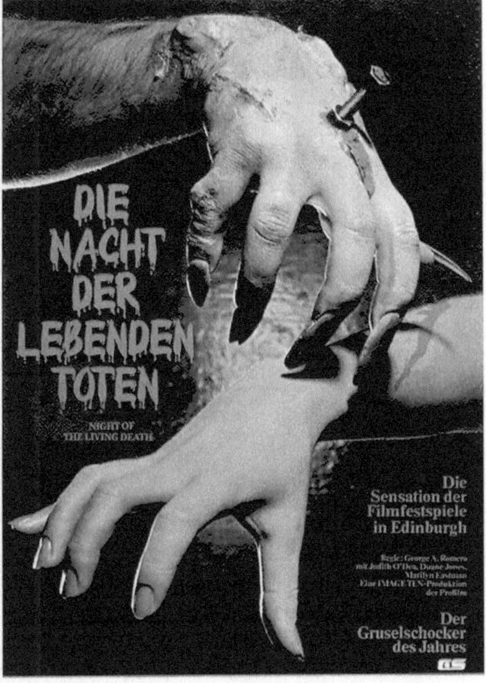

"The sensation of the Edinburgh Film Festival".

Before it's reputation bit, its first release in New York City was on a double-bill with *Dr Who and the Daleks*!

Rosemary's Baby, 1968 d. Roman Polanski p. William Castle

A William Castle production. The gimmick here is not ghosts or buzzed seats, insurance offers or a skeleton flying across the auditorium, but that rarest of things - the bloody good film. Roman Polanski blurs the edges of reality and fantasy, comfort and nightmare, so that the reality seems reassuringly sane and our heroine seems dangerously mad. Behind the scenes, just out of reach, diabolic deeds are afoot. Rosemary, the innocent, the never-seeking, the never-knowing, awakes to reality only when her part in the plot is over. Should she kill the baby with the horrible eyes? or should she rock it gently to sleep?

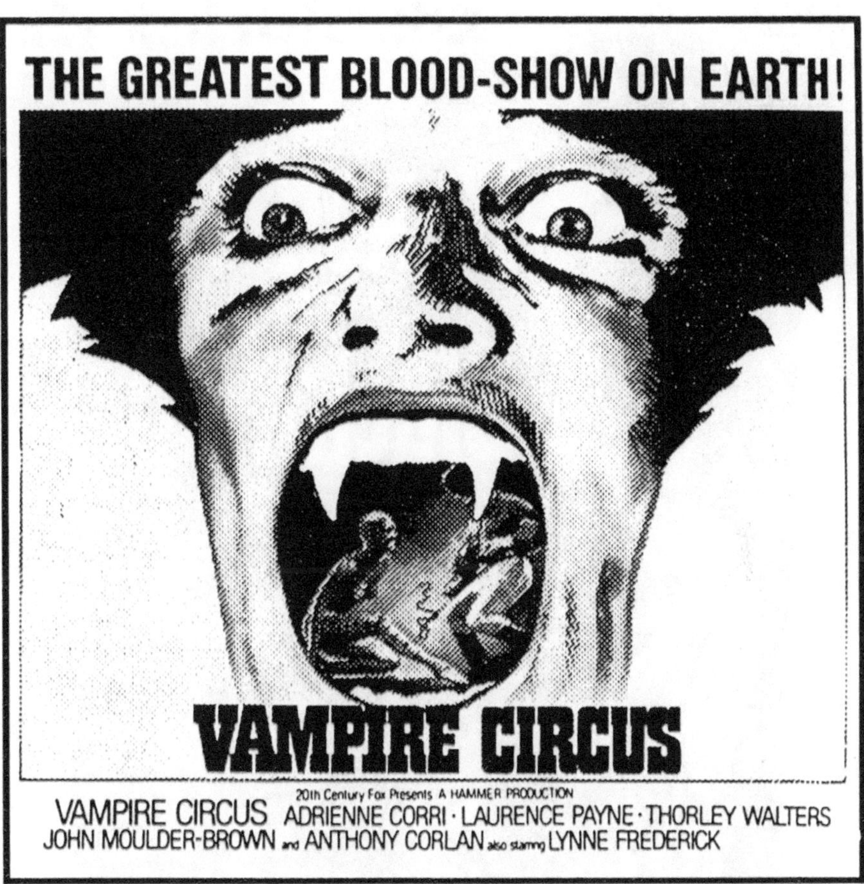

Vampire Circus, 1971 d. Robert Young p. Wilbur Stark

This advert will certainly cut through the clutter on a page of newsprint. I do like the presentation of the vampire fangs as a sort-of stage curtain, a metaphor for the doomed people (they are already inside the vampire's bite) but the ad doesn't convey the gorgeous gothic atmosphere of the violent, sadistic, fantastic and erotic film - a candidate for the best of the non-Peter Cushing Hammer horrors.

A vanquished vampire Count brings forth his gypsy cousin, Emil's Circus of Night, fronted by a white-faced dwarf (Skip Martin) and by a mute and shirtless David Prowse turning the handle of a music box. Big cats and bats turn into acrobats... and vampires. They're here to kill the children. Ex-child star Moulder-Brown is the improbable hero. Like *Usher*'s Mark Damon before him, he was whisked away to Italy by Count Luchino Visconti who cast him as mad *Ludwig*'s skinny-dipping cousin. A fine full-bodied orchestral score is matched here in the encircling forest scenes by an equally impressive use of atmospheric silence.

The Bloody Judge (Night of the Blood Monster), 1970
d. Jesús Franco p. Harry Alan Towers

Two fascinatingly different adverts. The German ad by Constantin-Film is the most truthful and the most alluring for an adult and adolescent audience. Re-titled *Night of the Blood Monster* by AIP in the States (right), the film was shorn of its S&M nudity and marketed for pre-teens, with a pleasant bit of bosom for dad in the accompanying Hammer horror main feature.
 'Blackmoor' was Edgar Wallace-speak for 'a dark and violent place in England'. See *Strangler of Blackmoor Castle* (qv).

Blood from the Mummy's Tomb, 1971 d. Seth Holt p. Howard Brandy

TERROR WAITS FOR YOU IN EVERY ROOM
in THE HOUSE THAT DRIPPED BLOOD x
From the author of "Psycho"
starring
CHRISTOPHER LEE · PETER CUSHING
NYREE DAWN PORTER · DENHOLM ELLIOTT · JON PERTWEE
with Joanna Dunham Joss Ackland John Bennett Wolfe Morris John Bryans
also starring TOM ADAMS and INGRID PITT as "Carla"
Produced by MAX J. ROSENBERG and MILTON SUBOTSKY Executive Producers PAUL ELLSWORTH
GORDON WESCOURT Screenplay by ROBERT BLOCH Directed by PETER DUFFELL AN AMICUS PRODUCTION
AND ·ONE OF THE 10 BEST PICTURES OF THE YEAR·
THE GUARDIAN
THE HONEYMOON KILLERS x
A WARREN STEIBEL PRODUCTION
Starring SHIRLEY STOLER · TONY LO BIANCO · MARY JANE HIGBY
Written and Directed by LEONARD KASTLE
NOW AT New Victoria OPPOSITE VICTORIA STATION TEL: 834-2544
ON GENERAL RELEASE AT SELECTED ODEON
AND OTHER LEADING CINEMAS FROM FEB. 21

HELD OVER MUST END NOV 3
"ONE OF THE GREAT SCUZZY MOVIES OF ALL TIME."
—JAMI BERNARD, NY POST
"A SUB-CELLAR NIGHTMARE."
—MICHAEL ATKINSON, NY PRESS
TONY LO BIANCO IN PERSON FRI 8 PM SHOW
THE HONEYMOON KILLERS
A WARREN STEIBEL PRODUCTION
Starring SHIRLEY STOLER · TONY LO BIANCO
Written and Directed by LEONARD KASTLE
WEDS-THURS 2, 4, 6, 8, 10 FRI-TUES 4, 8, 10

The House That Dripped Blood, 1971
d. Peter Duffell p. Milton Subotsky, Max Rosenberg

The house is leased from *A. J. Stoker and Co. from Hynde's Street, Braye* and comes with a copy of Lotte Eisner's book, *The Haunted Screen,* which gets a prominent close-up during the look-at-our-splendid-set-dressing title scene. Yes, the horror film went post-modern long before the self-reverential *Scream* (1996). This gently-paced starry cast chiller, with a flying Ingrid Pitt as the highlight, is a standard Amicus production. The opening tale about the screws turning a writer whose strangler story invades his personality, is Robert Bloch trying to reclaim his *Psycho* split personality trick that was so admired in *The Boston Strangler* (qv). Peter Cushing loses his head over a waxwork Salome. A cold Christopher Lee loses to his fire-frightened (witch) daughter. Jon Pertwee complains about the loss of realism in horror. If it's realism you want, bring on the second-half of the double-bill...

The Honeymoon Killers, 1970
d. Leonard Kastle p. Warren Steibel

This film about the banality of evil takes the form of a simple tale of a lonely woman (Shirley Stoler) finding love through a pen pal dating agency. She's a big attractive lady, powerful and sensitive, the matron in a hospital. The man she meets is a charmer, a Spaniard, with a portfolio of stolen hearts and a penchant for marriage. Hailed as a minor masterpiece (probably because Scorsese worked on it for few days before being sacked for being too slow). In truth, it's an effective film a few notches down from the full professional standard (e.g. the actors' pacing). It's the kind of film John Waters would have made then if he had to curb his wit and special treats.

The Anniversary, 1968
d. Roy Ward Baker p. Jimmy Sangster

Lust for a Vampire, 1971
d. Jimmy Sangster p. Michael Style, Harry Fine

And Soon the Darkness, 1970
d. Robert Fuest
p. Albert Fennell, Brian Clemens

Count Yorga, Vampire, 1970 d. Bob Kelljan p. Michael Macready

Ah, the good old German distributors re-titled the film *Young Blood for Dracula*, and put out press adverts that showed forth a lovely bit of nudity with the added promise, in the guise of a bat shaped and positioned almost like flung panties, that even more nudity was on show and in a sort-of 3D. In the States, the film itself was stripped away and released as a GP (PG).

Countess Dracula, 1971
d. Peter Sasdy p. Alexander Paal

Hell's Belles, 1969
d/p. Maury Dexter

Vehicles and horror always make a good team, from Dracula's horse-drawn carriage to an 18-wheeler truck that roars like Godzilla. Here's Amicus give a helping hand to a talented new director:

Asylum, 1972
d. Roy Ward Baker p. Milton Subotsky

Duel, 1971
d. Steven Spielberg p. George Eckstein

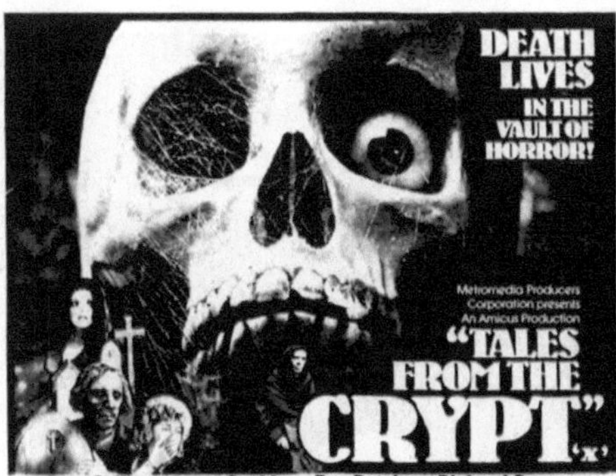

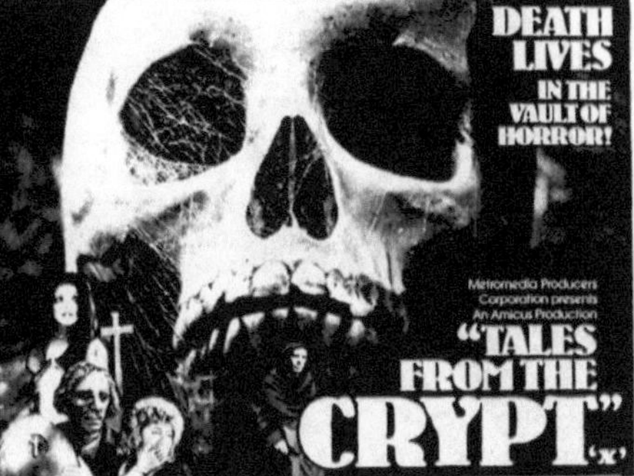

One in the eye for Amicus

AMICUS PRODUCTIONS, the specialists in multiple-decker horror films, have had a spot of trouble lately with censorship. Not with the good gentlemen of Soho Square, who seem to find their grisly goings-on quite acceptable under an X label, but with the powers that agree on what is fit for exhibition on public posters. The first Amicus snag came with the poster for Asylum which showed mad hands clawing at a set of faces that were placed inside the letters of the title. The design was found unsuitable for display on the London tube stations but later Paramount, the film's distributor, won a reprieve. Cinerama have not been so lucky with their eye staring from an empty skull socket to advertise Amicus's Tales From the Crypt. It was deemed all right for press advertising, but not by the London Transport Executive. So London's tube travellers are haunted by a gaping socket while all the major newspapers and billboards sport the glaring eye.

Tales from the Crypt, 1972
d. Freddie Francis
p. Milton Subotsky

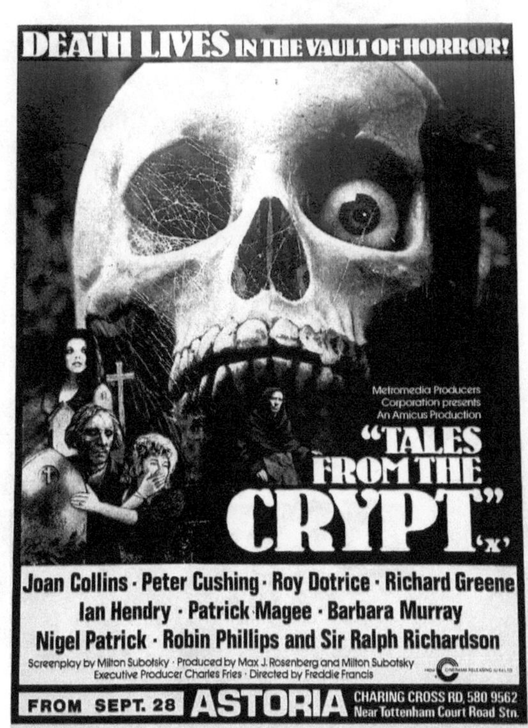

The word *cabinett* here conjours up memories of *Caligari*. In Germany, *House of Wax* was called *Das Kabinett des Professor Bondi*; *Scream and Scream Again* was re-titled *The Living Corpses of Dr. Mabuse*. Vincent Price is so Germanically perfect in these films that the distributors took to placing his characters and films into their own heritage.

The Abominable Dr. Phibes, 1971
d. Robert Fuest p. Ronald Dunas, Louis M. Heyward, exec-p. James H. Nicholson

Taking his cue from God's own book, an organist avenges himself on the medical staff who failed to save his wife. Comedy-horror of note for its Art-Deco sets and imaginative killings (death by self-tightening frog mask!) but Vincent Price's performance, in what was billed as his 100th film, is the reason to see it. Though burdened by heavy make-up and muteness (a disability that would nowadays all but guarantee him an Academy Award), his voice is heard only through an electronic gadget attached to his throat, but he still strikes the right balance of menace, humour and tragedy. The supporting players are mostly pantomime, enjoyable enough if you're in the mood to go with the flow, from the much loved Terry-Thomas (hand-cranking a film of a partially undressed dancer) to the Headmaster and pupil from Lindsay Anderson's *if....* (Peter Jeffrey, Sean Bury). Fuest directs in the comic strip style of his own TV's *The Avengers*: high-angle interiors shot through a fish-eye lens, low-angle exteriors filmed through roadside flowers.

The Thing with Two Heads, 1971
d. Anthony M. Lanza

A title change for the UK and new ad art

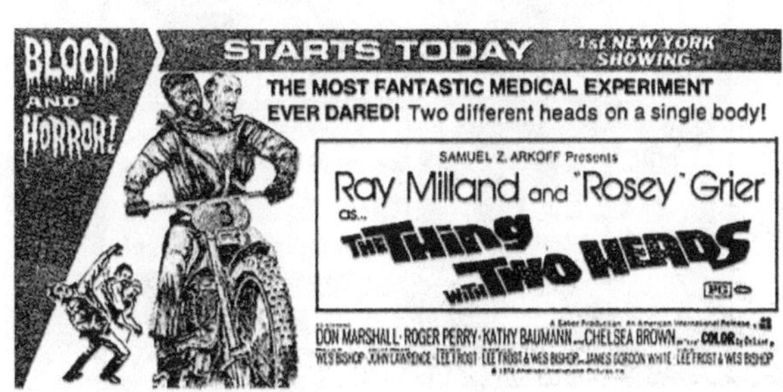

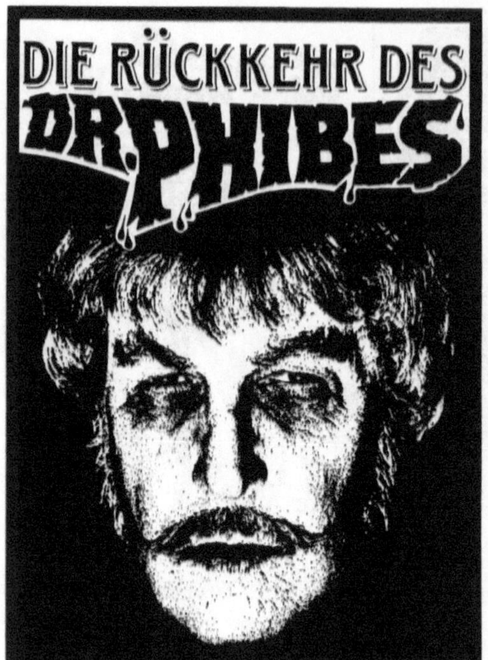

DR. PHIBES RISES AGAIN

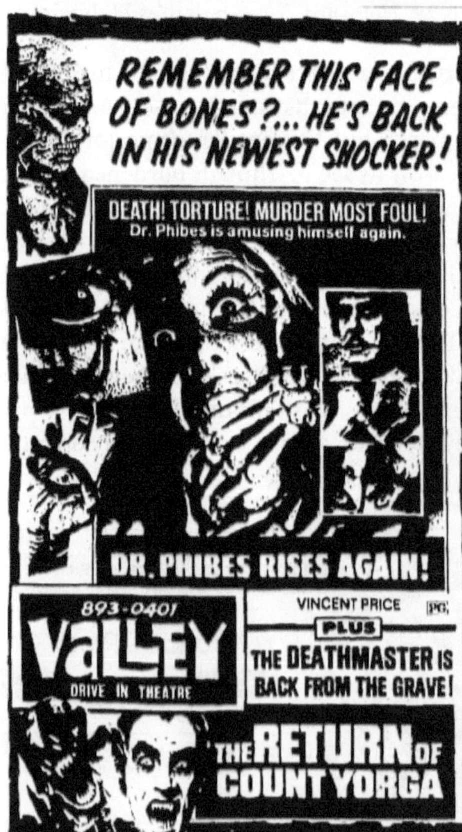

Dr. Phibes Rises Again, 1972
d. Robert Fuest p. Louis M. Heyward

The Return of Count Yorga, 1971
d. Bob Kelljan p. Michael Macready

Scream and Scream Again, 1970 d. Gordon Hessler
p. Max Rosenberg, Milton Subotsky, Louis M. Heyward

This is the film that scared me most, the one whose shocks jolted deepest, and I've only ever seen a third of it! I was an innocent but unsqueamish 12-year-old when this turned up on TV. As an infant I'd stayed overnight in a hospital and woken with a permanently damaged eye. I knew then that hospitals were places that *changed* you and not always for the better. When an ordinary and hitherto healthy fellow here wakes in a hospital bed with one of his limbs missing it took all my courage not to faint. Then Michael Gothard scratches the face off a beautiful woman and I'd seen more than enough. Gothard is best remembered as the loving-it Exorcist in *The Devils* (1971). As Tim Lucas first noted, he'd earlier cameoed un- credited in Ken Russell's magisterial *Isadora Duncan* (1966).

The first two Hammer films made entirely with British money.
They were budgeted at a lowly £200,000 each.

Dr. Jekyll and Sister Hyde, 1971 d. Roy Ward Baker p. Brian Clemens, Albert Fennell

Horror of Frankenstein, 1971 d. Roy Ward Baker p. Brian Clemens, Albert Fennell

Scars of Dracula, 1970 d. Roy Ward Baker p. Aida Young

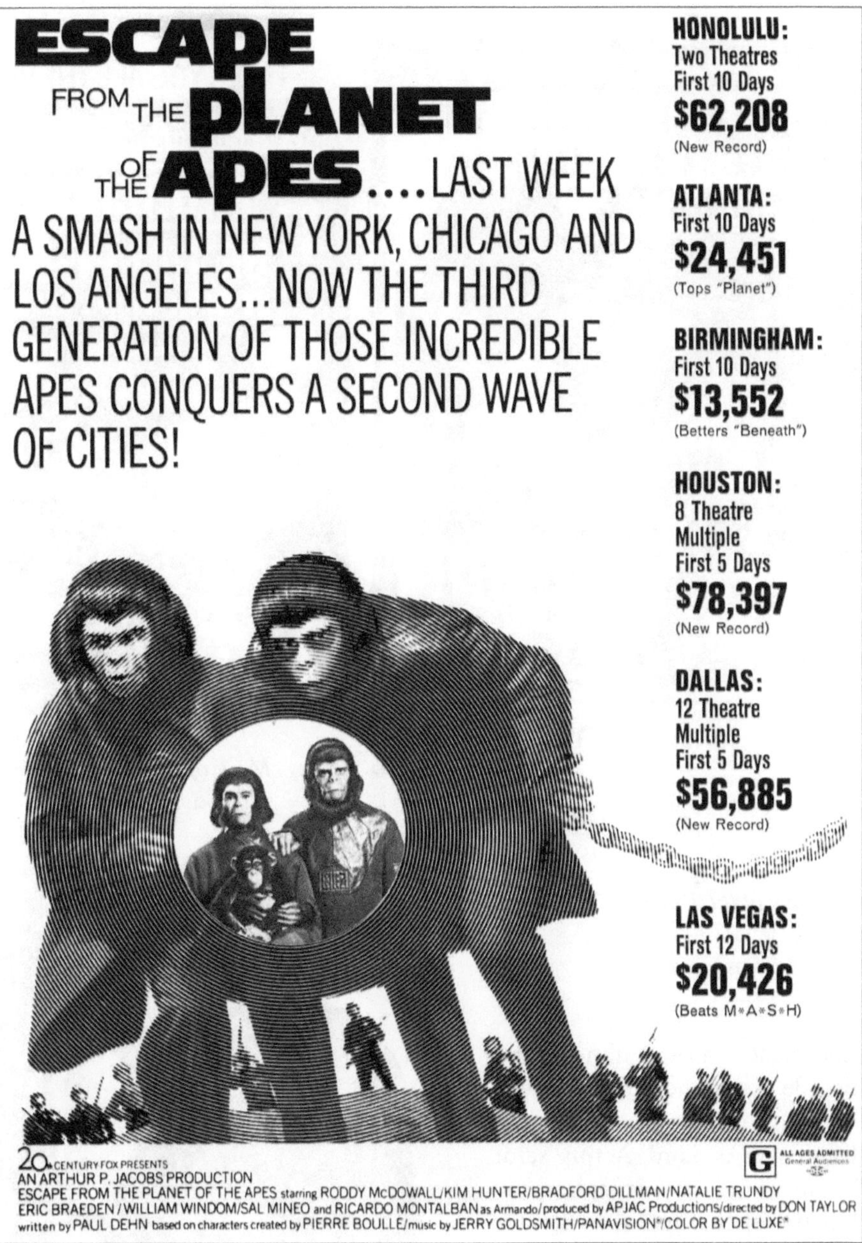

Escape from the Planet of the Apes, 1971 d. Don Taylor p. Arthur P. Jacobs

... And the world blows up and then there are three. Three apes left and three films made, and a fourth one about to be made, holding onto the bars of a cage in a travelling zoo and repeating one word which brings down all of mankind: "Mama. Mama. Mama."

Mark of the Devil 2, 1970
d/p. Adrian Hoven

Mark of the Devil, 1970
d. Michael Armstrong
p. Adrian Hoven

The most censored films of the decade were ones that shone a light on the crimes of the Establishment. As Lord Acton said: "Power tends to corrupt; absolute power corrupts absolutely."

The Devils, 1971 d. Ken Russell p. Robert H. Solo, Roy Baird

Ken Russell's film about an innocent man destroyed by a corrupt Church and State is the most powerful film ever made in England. Peerless direction, acting, design, editing and music. Russell's stature in 1971 was so high, with three first-run films about to be playing simultaneously in the West End, that *The Devil's* couldn't be suppressed there. It topped the London box-office for eight straight weeks. In the rest of England it played to massive crowds for a year and was the fourth highest grossing film of 1972, whereupon Warners did as Warners are wont to do when an 'investment' of theirs was about to go into profit, and mark a reduction in their 'take', they buried it as best they could, and through its heart they drove a stake.

Lindsay Anderson's first independent film, *O Dreamland!* (1953) was a 16mm short filmed in the Margate amusement park for which this advert was placed.

Web of the Spider (Nella stretta morsa del ragno), 1971
d. Antonio Margheriti   p. Giovanni Addessi

The Germans did like to use 'Dracula' in the titles of non-Dracula films. Here are a couple of non-Dracula films both using the iconography of a candelabra not as a sort of sexed-up cross but it makes for cheap set-dressing. This film, *Dracula in the Castle of Horrors,* is a remake of Margheriti's own *Danza macabra* (1963), but colour and Klaus Kinski fail to make up for the loss of Barbara Steele (with due respect to Michèle Mercier).

Vampyros Lesbos, The Heiress of Dracula, 1971 d. Jesús Franco p. Artur Brauner

If you are only allowed to keep one lesbian vampire film, write a polite and apologetic letter to Hammer's *The Vampire Lovers* (1970), which begat the early seventies rush, and perhaps choose this sunshine modernist beauty made mostly on location in Istanbul. Chose it not for its blood-red set dressing, red candles, red leather, a red kite flying, nor for its red raw illogicality (see a murder in the cellar? Smile and carry on with your day). But chose it to remember the dark tragic Soledad Miranda, bewitchingly gorgeous as a performance art vampire-stripper. The man in the ad is meant to be José Martínez Blanco, but in the film he has a perm and Michael Caine glasses.

The Bird with the Crystal Plumage, 1970 d. Dario Argento p. Salvatore Argento

I love the use of three-dimensional space in this exquisite press advert for a thrilling 35mm widescreen masterpiece. Dario Argento duly walked away with the Italian Golden Globes for best first feature and best new director. English Suzy Kendall and American Tony Musante give career-best performances. A perfectly preserved, though possibly snip-censored, 35mm print still screens now and then at the Bradford film museum. It looks nothing at all like the re-coloured bluray and is worth a long long journey to see, as is their print of...

Four Flies on Grey Velvet, 1971 d. Dario Argento p. Salvatore Argento

A simple direct image of a horrified woman reflected in the blade of a knife. An un-simple refection will provide the missing clue to the mayhem in *Deep Red* (1975), Dario Argento's next horror film. If we ignore Antonioni's *Blow-Up* (1966), from which came the star and a partial plot, was the British press ad (above) the spark for *Deep Red*? In any case it's a fabulous advert. It conveys a lot about Argento's style: a true understanding of physical space, of composition, close-up, silence, darkness, obliqueness, directness. That said, the UK ad was probably just a censor-friendly version of the American 'eyeball' ones:

Il cinema thrilling ha finalmente il suo capolavoro!

SCOPRIRAI CHE LA TUA PAURA CONFINA CON IL PROFONDO ROSSO...

Don't Look Now, 1971 d. Nic Roeg p. Peter Katz

That's $231,000 from tickets costing less than £1. This beautifully unsettling film about mourning has a finale as haunting as any, a dislocation of time as evocative as the finale to Chris Marker's *La Jetée* (1963). An architect (Sutherland) in Venice to work on the restoration of a church, sees his wife (Christie) in mourning dress on a funeral barge, although she is in fact in England with their young son who has hurt himself. The vision puts into motion a search for his wife that takes him into the city's hidden labyrinths where a serial killer is at work. The extended finale is linked to the film's opening sequence by content (Death) and by the explicit symbolism of water falling on water: a bucket of water thrown into a Venetian canal recreates the visual effect in the opening scene of rain drops falling on an English pond. The scenes are linked too by a red plastic raincoat worn in one by the victim, in the other by the killer.

The Nightcomers, 1971
d/p. Michael Winner

They're a dull lot, mostly, filmmakers. But Michael Winner had a sense of humour. I liked him for that. I admired him for assembling casts so starry they'd make M. G. and M. jealous, and I admired him for repeatedly standing up to the British censor (t'was Winner who told me that horrific tale about *Jaws*). He produced most of, and directed and edited all of, his own films (his modesty was such that he used a pseudonym for his editor credit). He also designed his own print ads. The one for *The Nightcomers* is par for the course, lashings of rave reviews, a wry wink because he never was the critics' darling. The repeating 'Brando' is an uncommon flourish. Directing Brando was the professional highlight of his life.

With the exception of a few of his Charles Bronson films, Winner's work hasn't yet reached the heights of cultdom, i.e. films that are adored. But he did have an accidentally massive influence on the horror genre, not with *The Nightcomers*, a surprisingly dull film of diction, greenery and breasts, but *The Sentinel* (qv), and not for it's hide-behind-your-hands parade of real freaks. *The Sentinel's* dislocated narrative, strange choices of camera lens, and massive box office success in Italy, woke the horror gene in Lucio Fulci and in Fulci's producers. In many ways, *The Sentinel* is the Fulci template.

Cinema TV Today 8/1/72
STEPHANIE BEACHAM originally planned to be a teacher of deaf children. Luckily for us, she was side-tracked into taking up an acting career which has proved very successful. Recently, she starred opposite Marlon Brando in "The Nightcomers." In her latest film for Hammer "Dracula A.D. 1972," she plays opposite Christopher Lee and Peter Cushing. Set in trendy London, Stephanie plays a fun-loving girl who innocently becomes entangled in Dracula's evil web. She joins the Hammer glamour parade as one of our girls to brighten up January.

BRANDO... BRANDO... BRANDO...
brilliant — stunning — captivating

ALEXANDER WALKER – EVENING STANDARD   DEREK MALCOLM – THE GUARDIAN   TIMOTHY FOOTE – TIME MAGAZINE

Eerily and effectively told...Winner's direction skilfully builds the story to a high pitch of suspense creating a mood and atmosphere which will haunt you for days. He draws fine performances from all his cast. Brando as Quint is superb.

CLIVE HIRSCHHORN – SUNDAY EXPRESS

A good effective film . . . has great visual beauty . . . Brando makes thoroughly believable both Quint's beguiling fascination for the children and his essential evil.
RICHARD MALLETT – PUNCH

An ingenious reworking of Henry James' story. The film exercises considerable fascination in every scene in which Brando appears . . . he is delightful . . . Stephanie Beecham is admirable . . . the children play up to them effectively.
PATRICK GIBBS – DAILY TELEGRAPH

A literate, cool, curiously spell-binding example of Victorian Gothic terror. Brando – totally in charge from first to last – a heavyweight performance.
BRUCE WILLIAMSON – PLAYBOY

No one who treasures inventive film-acting should miss it

MARGARET HINXMAN – SUNDAY TELEGRAPH

The screenplay is meticulously fashioned. Horrific is the word but it is horror refined . . . the writer, Michael Hastings and the director, Michael Winner, have done a fascinating job. The sensational aspect of it all has been astutely controlled.
GORDON GOW – FILMS & FILMING

An intelligent and provocative film, handsomely mounted and beautifully photographed. Michael Winner suggests skillfully the fierce and often hair-raising evil in the household and has leavened it with humour. It's without doubt Brando's best performance in a long time.
DAVID CASTELL – FILMS ILLUSTRATED

Stephanie Beecham is excellent, she conveys vividly the suppressed intensity of a passionate, perverse woman, cribbed, cabinned, and confined by the conventional lady like role forced on her by Victorian convention.
JOHN RUSSELL TAYLOR – THE TIMES

JOSEPH E. LEVINE presents
AN AVCO EMBASSY PICTURE

MARLON BRANDO
IN A MICHAEL WINNER FILM

Brando dominates with a brilliantly assembled portrait and Michael Winner's effective concept fills the film with things perversely out of place.

ALEXANDER WALKER – EVENING STANDARD

The NIGHTCOMERS x
STEPHANIE BEACHAM · THORA HIRD and HARRY ANDREWS

MUSIC BY JERRY FIELDING WRITTEN BY MICHAEL HASTINGS · PRODUCED & DIRECTED BY MICHAEL WINNER
AN ELLIOTT KASTNER · JAY KANTER · ALAN LADD JR · SCIMITAR PRODUCTION · COLOUR BY TECHNICOLOR · AN AVCO EMBASSY RELEASE

AT SELECTED ODEON AND OTHER IMPORTANT THEATRES
N. LONDON FROM OCT 29 · S. LONDON FROM NOV 5

Straw Dogs, 1971 d. Sam Peckinpah   p. Daniel Melnick

<u>An Imaginary Discussion</u>
<u>at the Print Publicity Department</u>

Man 1: "Yes, I know she's lovely but we don't need to see her face. She's just a pair of tits to them, you see? I'll zoom in on her tits, her nipples poking through the sweater. And I'll put a picture of the man on her tits, with his long erect gun out and about to explode all over them. It shows the rape without showing it. If you know what I mean?"

Man 2: "He's her husband?"

Man 1: "Is he?"

Man 2: "And besides, you'll never get away it."

In the UK it was sold as violent sex "red raw rape" . In the USA it was sold as a sort-of Charles Atlas course on violence and vengeance.

Shivers, 1971 d. David Cronenberg p. Ivan Reitman

A mad doctor creates a synthetic parasite that reduces brain power and increases the sex drive. The dead rise up and attack the living. Before George Romero gave us Monroeville Mall as the ultra new oasis for a ghoul-infested present, Cronenberg gave us this B-movie Ballardian tale of a mutant venereal disease sweeping through a Montreal island high rise. He even throws in a sex-fuelled car crash.

In the States, the film shivered off the timbers of the terrible title to go with *They Came from Within*, and also *The Parasite Murders*. The parasites here being the men who pray on young girls, the salesmen and the insurance brokers who pray on decent folks, and the scientists playing God with government grants. The parasites are also a rubbery ribbed penis-sized monster that burst from a man's stomach (Dan O'Bannon are you watching?). Cronenberg reworked images of stomach-birth for years.

The Queen of European horror herself, Barbara Steele, plays an underwritten support role, head back and smoking, then swigging wine, now having a bath (that *is* meant to be her in the adverts) and, er, having a lesbian kiss and swim. She looks like a giant here. Cronenberg was clearly working through an adolescent fantasy.

Werewolf's Shadow, 1971 d. León Klimovsky p. Salvadore Romero

Horror Express 1972 d. Eugenio Martín
p. Bernard Gordon

Here the American distributors get it right where the
Germans get it wrong. That shapeless fudge of a monster on the German ad does the film no favours. The
ad for the screening at the Florida drive-in is a perfect
piece of fun. The film itself is a byword for pleasure.
Cushing and Lee are at their peerless best. Savalas, all
sheepskin and energy, bounds onto the screen with
more gusto and star presence than ever he mustered
outside of *Kojak*.

The Dead Are Alive, 1972   d. Armando Crispino p. Artur Brauner

A dark advert of a hooded living dead zombie (the costume and attitude that clearly influenced youth and youth fashion these last couple of decades) with an amusing sketch of ... is that really Samantha Eggar?

Theatre of Blood, 1973 d. Douglas Hickox p. Gustave Berne, Sam Jaffe

The second of Vincent Price's on-location-in-Putney films (after *Scream and Scream Again*). It brings down and burns up the curtain of the old Putney Hippodrome on a sort-of loose London Tramps Trilogy with *A Clockwork Orange* and *O Lucky Man!* both of which feature scenes in a theatre (though *Theatre of Blood* is not nearly in the same league as the Kubrick and the Anderson). Cinematographer Wolfgang Suschitzky shows off some remarkable full focus wide-angle photography. His son, Peter, would soon be working wonders with Ken Russell and David Cronenberg. Douglas Hickox's son, Anthony, directed *Hellraiser 3*. Coincidentally, the set-dressing includes two very large and ugly birds with crystal plumage. A nod to Dario?

137

Frankenstein and the Monster from Hell, 1974 d. Terence Fisher p. Roy Skeggs

David Prowse. Wow! From posing in speedos to Hammer to *A Clockwork Orange* to *Star Wars* to training *Superman* (and all that before I reached the age of ten!). He was frozen out of official *Star Wars* functions by Lucas for questioning the creative accounting that claimed the *Star Wars* sequels failed to make a profit, robbing him of due payments. But in the UK, the 501st State stood by Prowse and rightly made him their Commander in Chief.

Tombs of the Blind Dead, 1972 d. Amando de Ossorio

Return of the Blind Dead, 1973 d. Amando de Ossorio

The Ghost Galleon, 1974 d. Amando de Ossorio

A curious trilogy of ads (above). The first two compare the film to the most brutal films of the genre. The third references Disney and says *The Blind Dead* is a kids film.

Creature with the Blue Hand, 1967 d. Alfred Vohrer p. Horst Wendlandt

Before Freddy Krueger's clawed glove became a defining image of the 1980s horror film, there was a small flurry of steel-clawed gauntlets in the late 60s early 70s cinema, most effectively in Bruce Lee's *Enter the Dragon* (1973).

Wenn der Dämon erwacht...

When the Demon awakens...

DÄMON des GRAUENS
(CRAZE)

JACK PALANCE · TREVOR HOWARD
DIANA DORS

„Ich weiß nun, daß ich doch nicht
so abgebrüht bin, wie ich dachte!"
Volker G., Wien   'I know now that I'm not as
brave as I thought!'

„Wenn ich jetzt in den Keller gehe,
muß ich immer pfeifen!"
Franz R., Essen

'If I go down to the cellar now,
I always have to whistle!'

„Es war wie ein böser Traum
und ich konnte
nicht aufwachen!"
Susanne L., Düsseldorf

'It was like a bad dream and I could not wake up!'

„Ich hatte ganz einfach
entsetzliche Angst!"
Ute A., Hamburg

'I was just terrified!'

Death Walks at Midnight, 1972
d/p. Luciano Ercoli

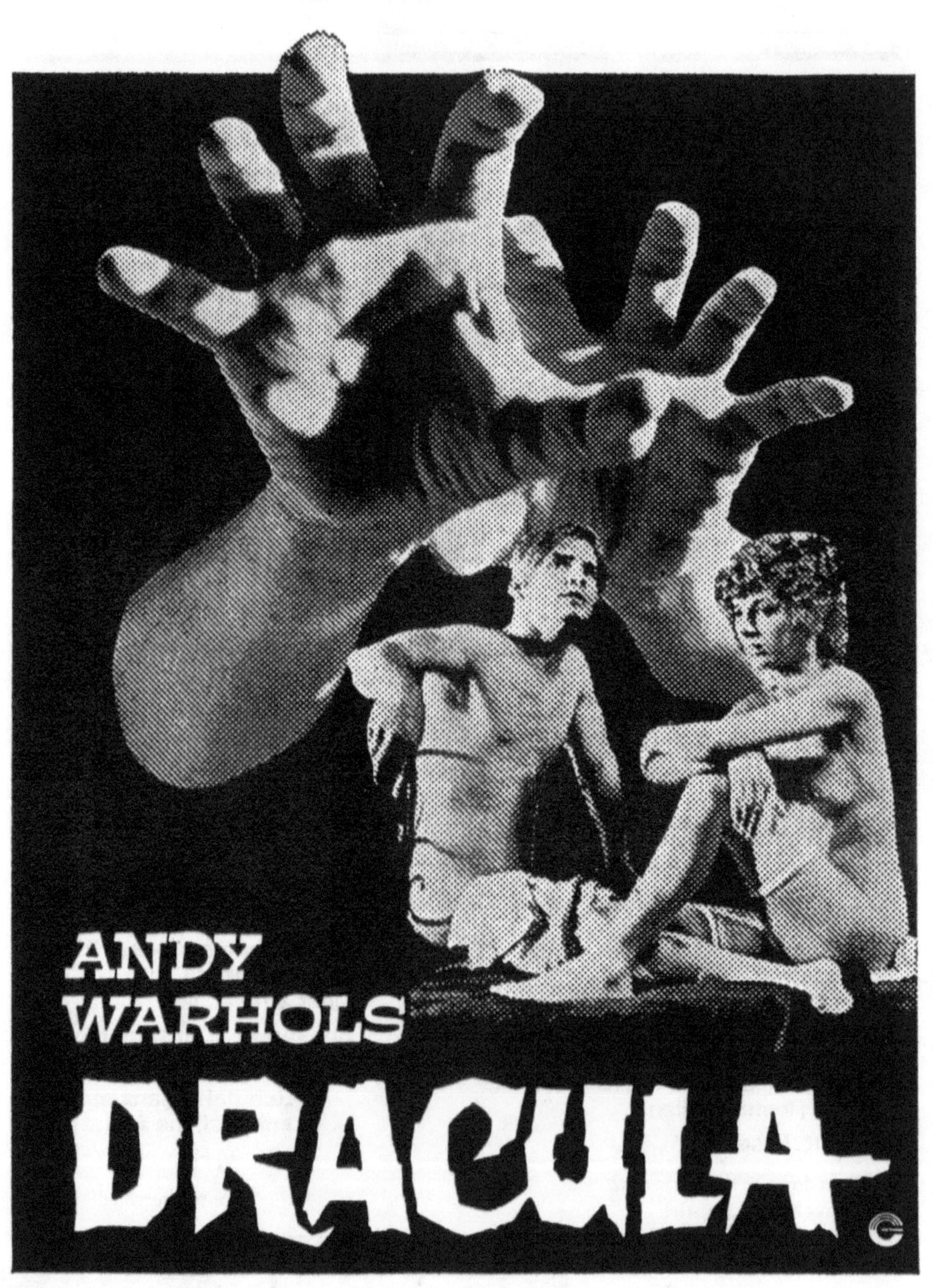

Blood for Dracula, 1974 d. Paul Morrissey p. Carlo Ponti

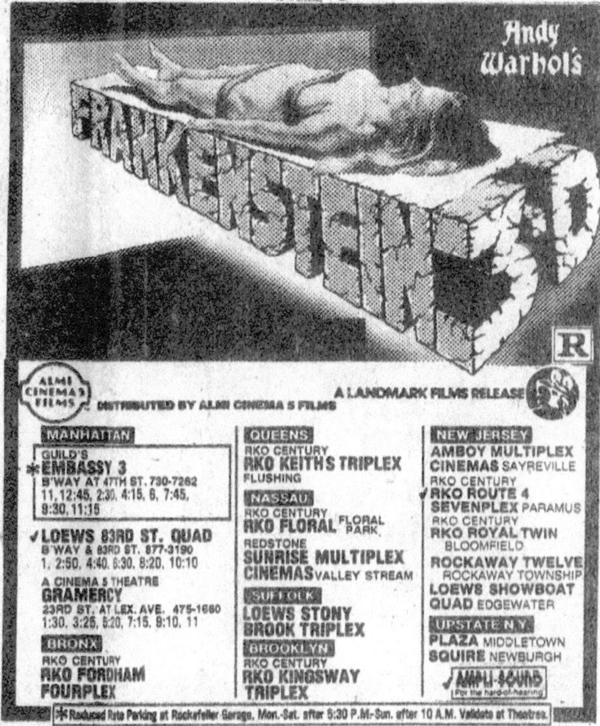

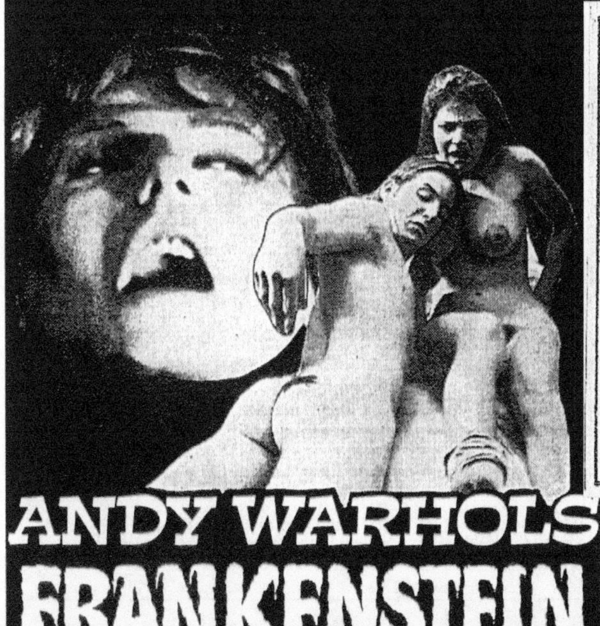

Flesh for Frankenstein, 1973
d. Paul Morrissey
p. Carlo Ponti

The Wicker Man, 1973 d. Robin Hardy p. Peter Snell

Last House on the Left, 1972 (advert from 1975)
d. Wes Craven p. Sean S. Cunningham

Rare non-Von Sydow imagery for the 1974 UK press adverts

The Exorcist, 1973 d. William Friedkin p/sc. William Peter Blatty

A horror film so effective that The Imbecilia (the British censors) banned it from home video for 13 years from 1986! The film succeeds because the sensational theme, the demonic possession of a girl, is presented in a manner so straight that, until the special effects finale, *The Exorcist* could be said to have docu-drama pretensions. It opens in an alien landscape, an Iraqi desert of light and colour and space (photographed by Billy Williams) to be contrasted with the cold, cramped interiors of a house in Georgetown, USA (photographed by Owen Roizman). Nothing much happens for the first forty minutes, lots of little filler scenes, hollow snapshots of the character's lives, then the girl announces her illness by urinating on the floor. The sheer boldness of the possession scenes take one by surprise. The soundtrack, which had offered up all manner of amplified sounds, barking dogs, screeching tube trains, ringing telephones, does its utmost to scare us.

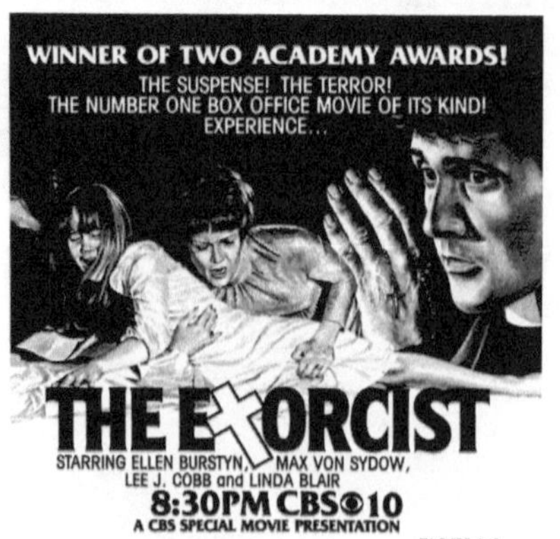

70mm! with two-extra tracks of sound!

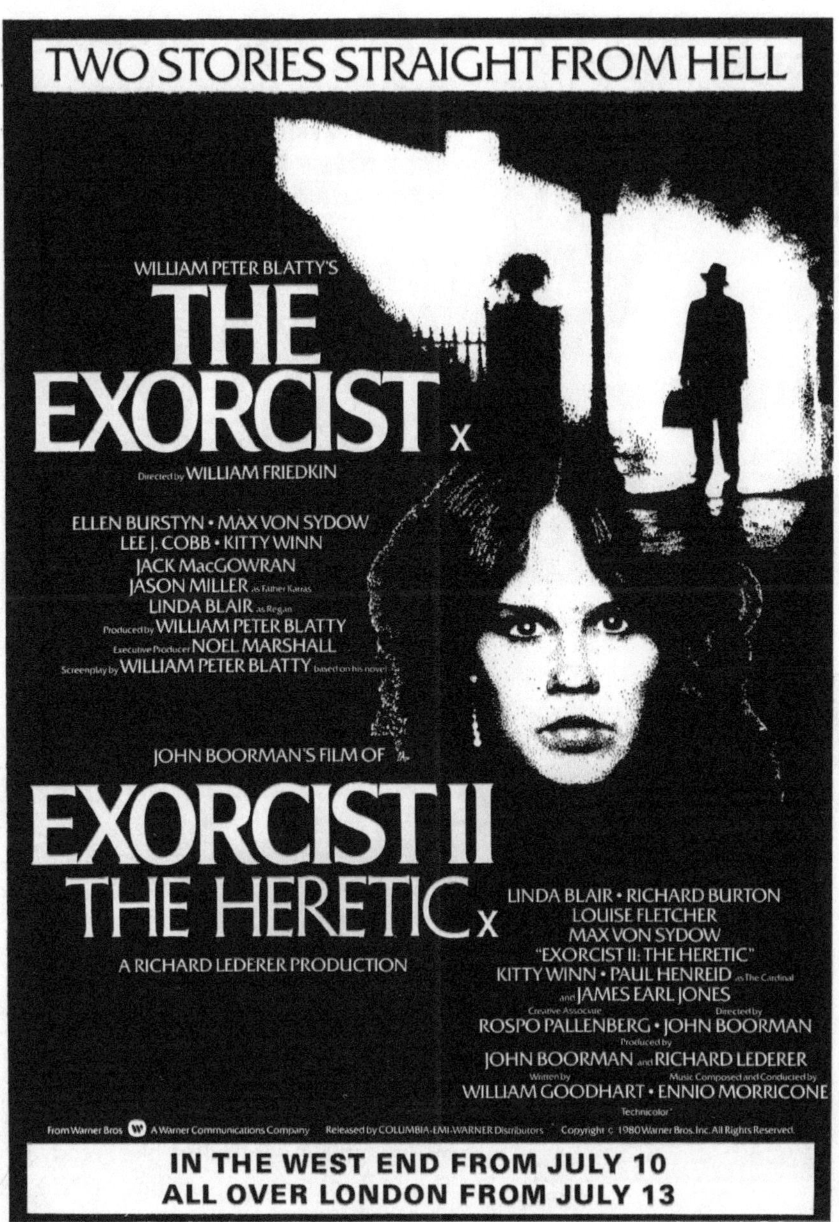

Exorcist II, The Heretic, 1977 d/p. John Boorman

Of all the strange unexplainable facts about *The Exorcist,* and they are legion, the most disturbing is that Martin Scorsese included *Exorcist II* in his *Guilty Pleasures* piece in *Film Comment* (Sept. 78). He said it is a better film than the original. I think he used the word 'masterpiece'.

  This advert hails from 1983 and duly had me and my school friends encamped in the stalls at the St. Helens ABC during that summer of double-bill marvels: *Dirty Harry* and *The Enforcer, House by the Cemetery* and *The Beyond, Lemon Popsicle* twinned with our particular favourite, *Flesh Gordon.*

Still screening six years later.

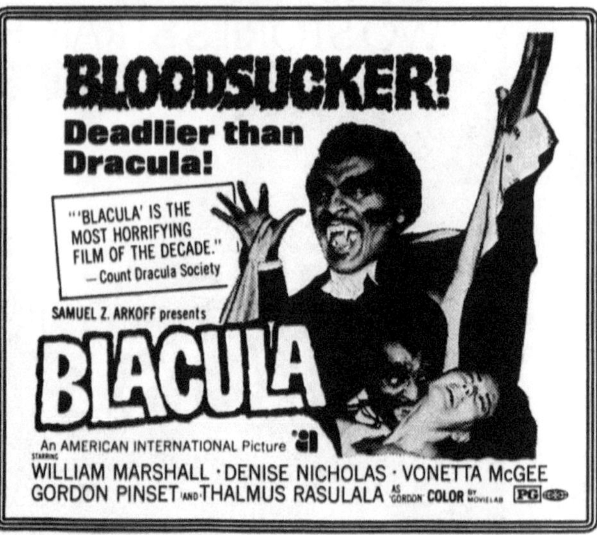

Blacula, 1972 d. William Crain p. Joseph T. Naar

Abby, 1974 d/p. William Girdler

Black Frankenstein, 1973
d. William A. Levey p/sc. Frank R. Saletri

Voodoo Black Exorcist, 1974
d. Manuel Caño p. J.A. Pérez Giner

Blacula's William Marshall unearths an ebony box in Nigeria that releases a demon (voiced by Bob Holt and sounding like Freddy Krueger). This blaxploitation version of *The Exorcist* played to sell-out audiences for 10 weeks before being pulled from the theatres and buried with a wooden stake in its release book, presumably hammered in by lawyers in the employ of Warner Brothers. Not a well-made film. It's by the young white Jewish maestro of *Grizzly*. Speaking of bold white Jewish blaxploitation trailblazers, next up is a massive box-office hit by the *Black Caesar* godfather himself ...

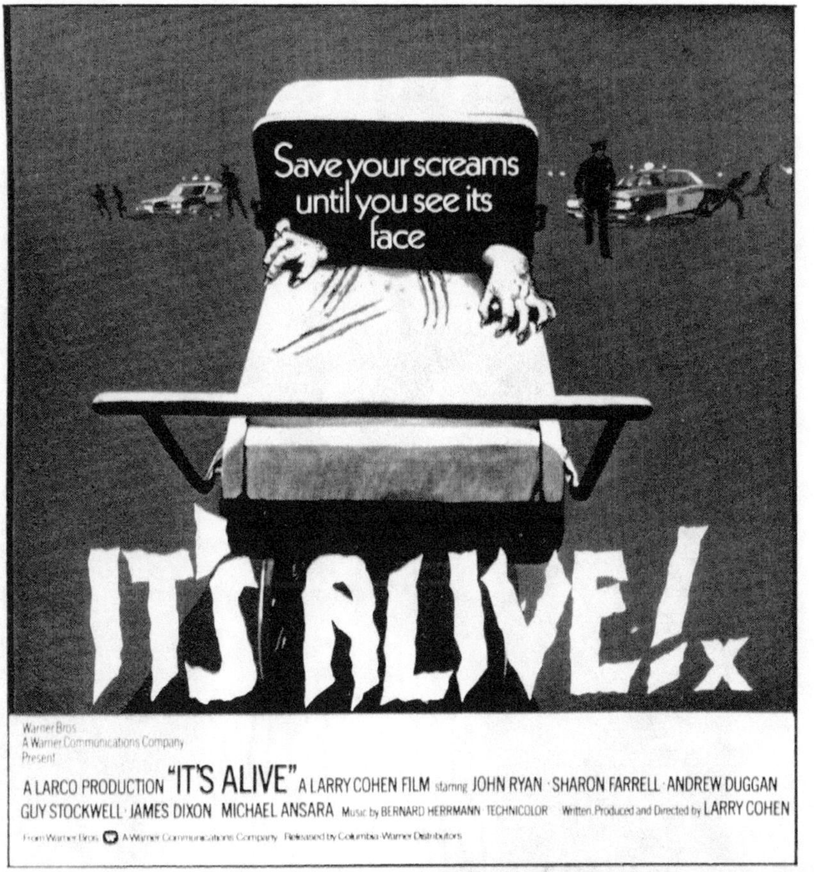

It's Alive, 1973 d/p/sc. Larry Cohen

The UK ad-line tells us that the distributors saw *Rosemary's Baby* and loved it. The USA 1977 re-release ad-line (right) is among the best ever written. The opening scenes of a loving family on the eve of the birth of a baby are staged and acted with such intelligence they mark out Larry Cohen as a major talent. He could have been a John Hughes of the Seventies if his imagination hadn't been so black. Fenton Hamilton's low-light full palette photography is as impressive as any in a horror film of the period (he won two technical Oscars for his developments in lighting). But when the horror starts, the leading players react by losing their sparkle and subtlety, and Cohen's imaginative staging and writing dry up. The whole tumbles down to B-movie level. Fittingly, Ryan was cast from a Broadway production of *Medea*.

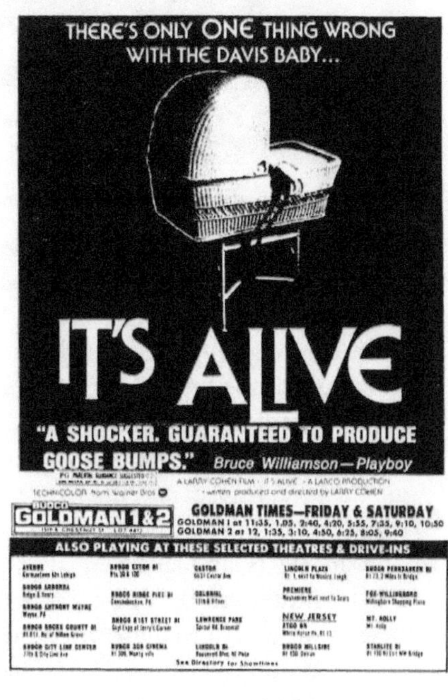

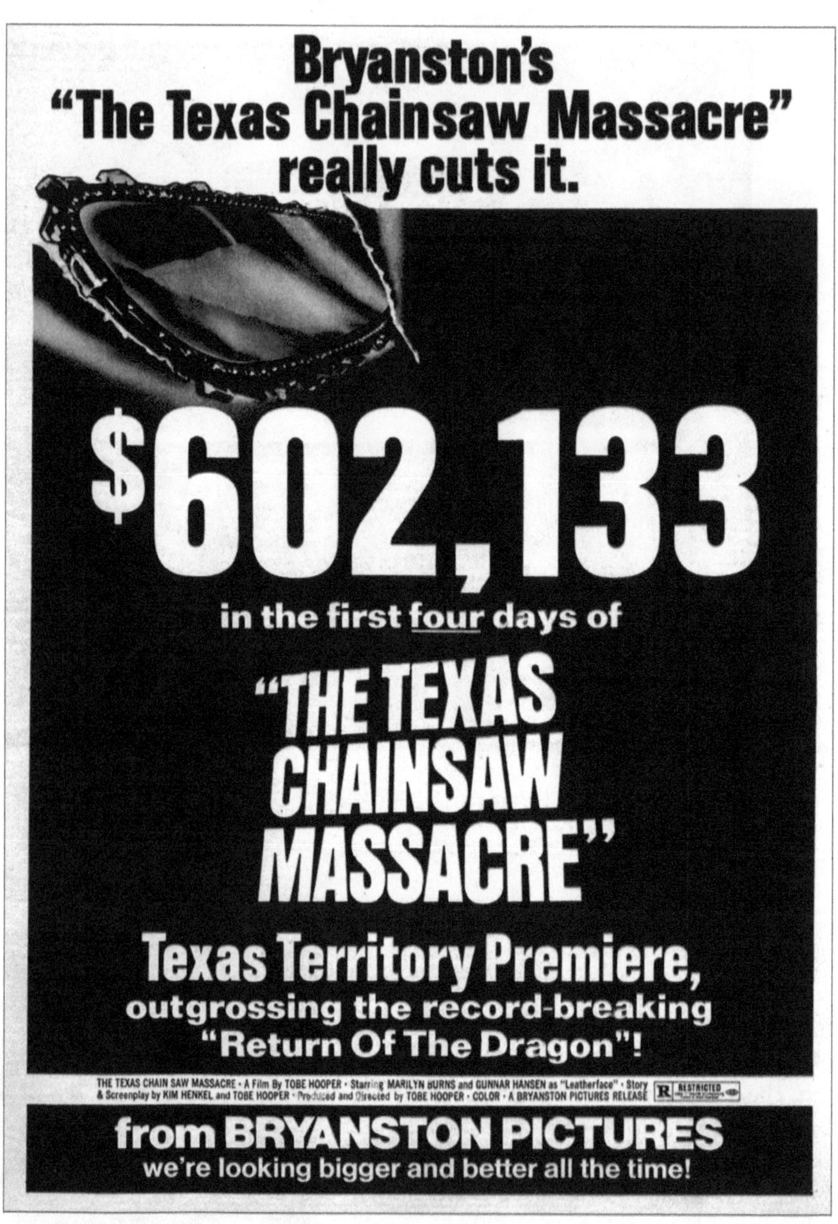

It took a long long time for the money to filter through to the cast. Remember the frostiness of the first DVD commentary? Gunnar Hansen, with decades of financial cheatery still rankling him, could barely bring himself to be in the same room as Tobe Hooper. Then the fan conventions really started to rise and the cast began to get the love, respect and the money they richly deserve. The signs of the robbery were there in this the first post-release trade press ad. No mention is made of the makers. The ad starts and ends by trumpeting 'Bryanston', the distributors. In Michael Doyle's indespensible book, *Larry Cohen The Stuff of Gods and Monsters*, Cohen says Bryanston was "a Mafia-owned organisation and, eventually, they were investigated and went out of business." Creative accounting, including voluntary bankruptcy, are favoured ways corrupt business folk steal profits.

The Texas Chainsaw Massacre (1974)
d/p/sc/ed & truly outstanding music score, Tobe Hooper

The Redeemer, 1978 d. Constantine S. Gochis p. Sheldon Tromberg

An enjoyably pretentious wraparound wraps around six 'best of year' folks at a High School reunion. T. G. Finkbinder is a solidly effective villain going through guises and accents as if he's a small town Vincent Price in a college production of *Theatre of Blood.*

Friday the 13th: The Orphan, 1977 d/p/sc John Ballard

The Orphan, filmed-over-ten-years, fails to break from its all too amateur style. In the restored version, every scene is too long or too short. Beda Batka's Czech-style photography is consistently mis-used. For example, a low-angled close-up at a mourner at a graveside, with a backdrop of trees nicely out of focus, is repeated five or six times as the director insists on padding the scene by showing everyone in turn standing round the grave, while a Janis Ian song plays competingly on the soundtrack. A rich man's small son inherits his country house, his druggy African friend, a controlling aunt and a stuffed chimpanzee. A rotund uncle with a twinkle in his eye gives the boy an elephant gun. There isn't any horror until the end. Stephen Thrower (over) champions the released version in his landmark book, *Nightmare USA*, from which I've taken the ad.

Legend of the Witches, 1970 d. Malcolm Leigh p. Olive Negus-Fancey

Jaws, 1975 d. Steven Spielberg p. Richard D. Zanuck, David Brown

Harking back to the "Roll-up! Roll-up!" days of film as a carnival attraction, ad-lines are often memorable, boastful, creative and false. Here's a rare one that tells only the truth. I can imagine the advertising team beaming with pride. They certainly came up with a wry one for *Jaws 2.*

Jaws is the goriest and the most frightening film ever granted a certificate for viewing by children and my how the children loved it! That said, the diabolical British censor took an idiot's pride in refusing it a certificate until every single print, of the 520 or so that had been made for the UK, were damaged by having several frames ripped out. Less than a second all told but just enough to make the picture jump, and just enough so that the censor could boast he had damaged it and shown off his power. That real-life horror, of a fool putting a perverse private pleasure before public good, and a crime against art, echoes the main theme of the film's plot line of authorities putting private profit before public safety. *Jaws* is a film of two equal parts. Part One details the town and its problem (a shark, a mayor). Part Two follows the adventures of three men in a boat. They do need a bigger boat.

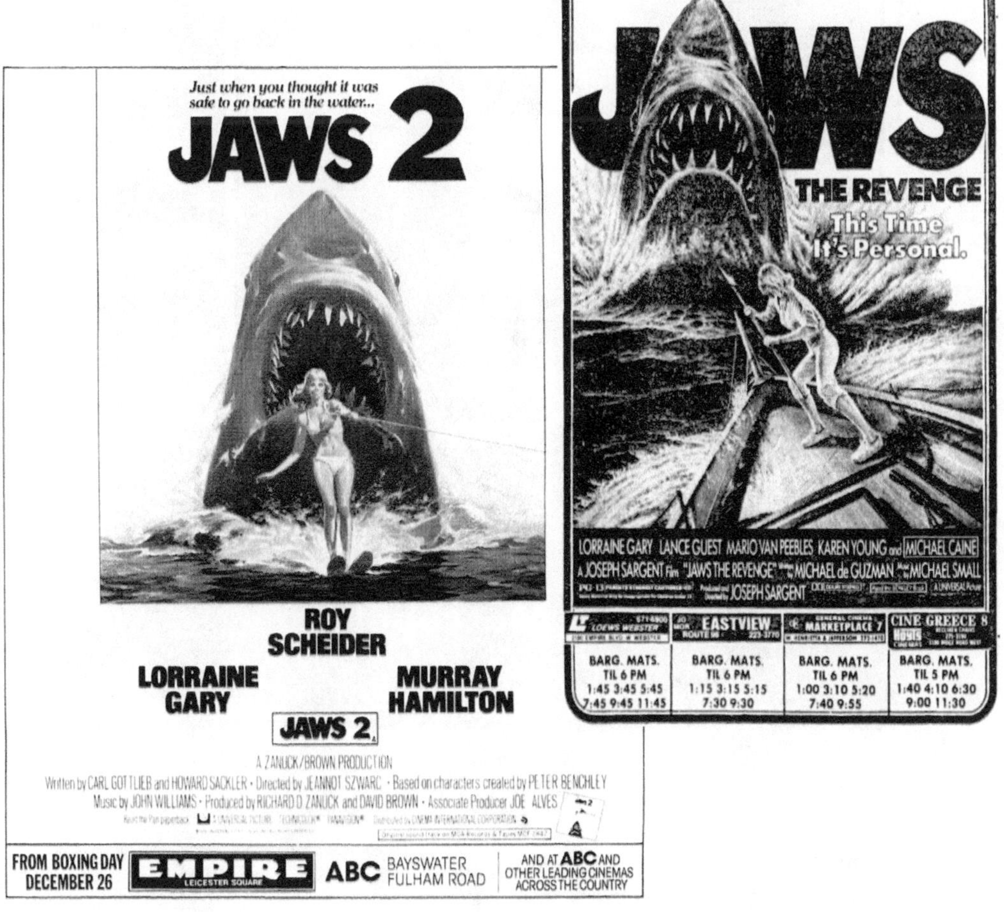

Jaws 2, 1978 d. Jeannot Szwarc p. Richard D. Zanuck, David Brown
Jaws the Revenge, 1987 d/p. Joseph Sargent

Grizzly, 1976 d/p. William Girdler

The film's main assets are a Todd-AO camera system and a helicopter. Both put to good use. *Grizzly* was the talk of the playground when it came out, a friend reporting truly and breathlessly that the bear "decapitates a horse!". Bizarrely, Girdler himself was decapitated in a helicopter accident.

King Kong, 1976 d. John Guillerman p. Dino De Laurentiis

I was only a tiny kid when I first saw this ad for Dino's *King Kong* but I knew that adline was bollocks. Dino De Laurentiis. What a producer! You have to admire a man who had the Italian Southern border moved so that his film studio could qualify for government grants. In addition to finding the tens of millions of dollars to make and market *Kong*, Dino's main contribution was to insist that a 50-foot robot gorilla be built, covered with real animal fur, and used irregardless of the cost. The 50-foot Kong isn't seen much in the film. It doesn't look real but it does look fantastic. It had me gasping with joy when I saw it in one of the huge (now deceased) Lime Street cinemas in Liverpool. This ad is for screenings at London's massive and newly ex-Cinerama cinema - the Casino. *Kong* inaugurated Dino's Trilogy of Giant Mechanical Beasts, with Charles Bronson providing the muscle for *White Buffalo* (1977) and Richard Harris ever impressive as he takes on *Orca The Killer Whale* (1977). I like the films' combination of fake Felliniesque sets with good old Hollywood-style locations and acting.

The Food of the Gods, 1976
d/p/spfx. Bert I. Gordon

With box office bells tolling from a big shark, a big bear and a big-big ape, B.I.G. Bert rolled up his sleeves, encamped to Bowen Island and gave us his masterpiece, having made a career out of a genuinely effective photographic effect that enabled B.I.G. creations to be more lifelike than the beasts of his bigger budgeted peers. Here he fills a barn with giant chickens then he fills a forest with rats the size of lions. He blows them apart with a shotgun, for real! The climactic shot of a river of giant rats surrounding our heroes on the roof a farm house is the single most impressive 'big beasts' moment in all 70s cinema. Almost as impressive is the fact that the three leading ladies - Ida Lupino, Pamela Brown, Belinda Balaski - are not used as B-movie T&A (that was left to the ad agency). Balaski and some of the crew were hired in from *Locusts* (1974), a nature-runs-amuck TV Movie of the Week.

I first saw *The Food of the Gods* on 16mm, projected to a happy crowd of adolescents packed into the Victorian Gothic town hall in St. Helens. The girls screamed. The boys laughed. A fine fun night to remember. But for all the big beastery, the film is linked closer still to the decade span of horror art protest films on environmental themes. The 70s were a dirty decade indeed, from leaded petrol to unchecked industrial pollution. Our city walls were streaked black with acid rain. Lacking a politician like Al Gore to shine a light on inconvenient truths, bands of genre filmmakers used screen gore instead - from *Doomwatch* (1972) to *Piranha* (1978) and *Prophecy* (1979).

Q: What links *The Food of the Gods* to *The Rocky Horror Picture Show*?

A: Grant Wood's *American Gothic* painting features in both.

The Rocly Horror Picture Show, 1975
d. Jim Sharman p. Michael White

Younger readers will probably find it hard to believe that transsexuals and transvestites from Transylvania were once considered oddities and were confined to the darkest corners of society. Now it's Route One to a job at the BBC and to an Arts Council grant. This beloved film, made at Hammer's Bray Studios from a Royal Court Theatre collection of love songs to seminal genre films, is given heart and style by Tim Curry's bewitchingly wry performance and by his beautiful voice. But when a film selling itself on sex and horror is given an AA rating (suitable for children aged 14 and over) and not an adults only 'X', the advertisers stepped in to hoodwink the public with the star shaped as a big raunchy 'X'.

Rare pre-film ad for the play.

1983 Torrance, California

Phantom of Paradise, 1974
d. Brian De Palma
p. Edward R. Pressman

Carrie, 1976 d. Brian De Palma
p. Paul Monash

From a trickle of blood in sensuous slow-motion showers under penis-shaped shower heads to a long slow-motion tease of a high bucket of blood held by a rope. The characters are sketched large and true and the plot is clean and direct. A terrible deed is set up and, with notice posted long before it happens, suspense comes naturally as the time to showdown ticks away. De Palma shows off an impressive slow-motion camera choreography in a delicious seven-minute slow dance that ends with the real-time tug of the rope. The supporting cast of twenty-something teenagers from (Norman) Bates High provide expertly stage-managed grins, giggles and screams. Two years later, John Travolta was STILL in high school in *Grease*. Here he drives in in a scene copied from *American Graffiti*. He was reunited with the ever fine Nancy Allen in De Palma's excellent *Blow Out*.

Race With the Devil, 1976
d. Jack Starrett p. Wes Bishop

Schizo, 1976
d/p. Pete Walker

Deliverance in a camper van that builds to a dry run for the chase finale of *Mad Max 2*. There's one erotic black mass, two meaty rattlesnakes, and a chillingly good turn of the suspense screw. R.G. Armstrong impresses in a layered performance as the Sheriff, but where's Barry Newman when you need him to pop a few pills and drive the hell away?

Hands of the Ripper, 1971 d. Peter Sasdy p. Aida Young

The German title of this Hammer horror is *Hands full of blood*. The ad carries a lurid image of an unconscious woman about to be penetrated by a madman's knife. Look at the tension in that hand! Alas the film, rated PG in the States, doesn't live up to the poster. Not so the 1976 film on the same theme (right). There's no need for gore and sex imagery to sell a Jack the Ripper film when the monster is played by a star actor as thrillingly alive as Klaus Kinski.

Jack the Ripper, 1976 d. Jesus Franco p. Erwin C. Dietrich, Max Dora

And now this fine devil's daughter …

To the Devil a Daughter, 1976
d. Peter Sykes p. Roy Skeggs

Pushed into production by Lee through his own production company, Charlemagne, in alliance with Rank and Hammer. This £350,000 film seems cherishably sexual when you watch it on TV as a 14-year old but it's a shoddy shapeless mess when re-visiting it in middle age. Widmark persuaded Lee to advance his career by moving to the States. *Saturday Night Live*, *Airport '77* and *1941* quickly followed in the slow-slow-slow rise to *Star Wars* prequels and *The Lord of the Rings*. In her three most major films, *Tess* ('79), *Paris, Texas* ('84) and *Revolution* ('85), Kinski is perfectly miscast and still perfect.

The Omen, 1976
d. Richard Donner
p. Harvey Bernhard

Damien, Omen 2, 1978
d. Mike Hodges, Don Taylor
p. Harvey Bernhard

The Final Conflict, 1981
d. Graham Baker
p. Harvey Bernhard

Suspiria, 1976 d. Dario Argento p. Claudio Argento

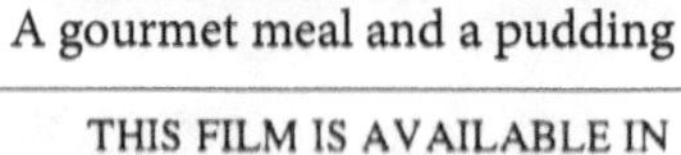

A gourmet meal and a pudding

1989 VHS advert

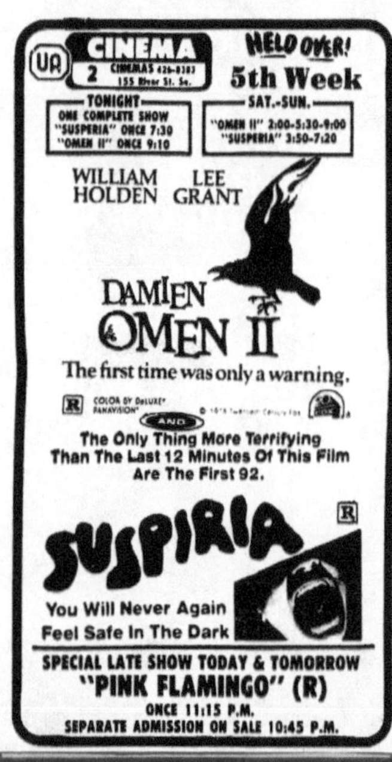

We paid a lot for our collections

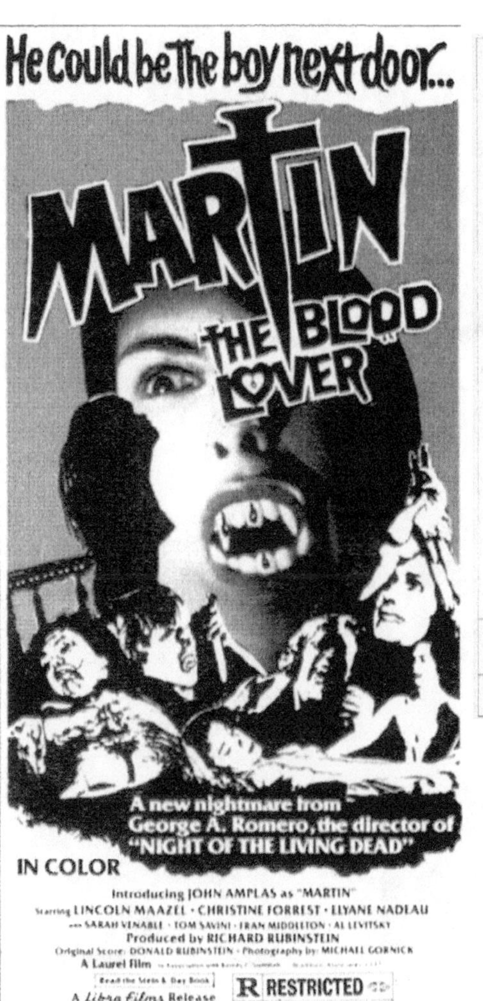

Martin, 1977
d. George A. Romero
p. Richard Rubinstein

The first George Romero film to be special effected by Tom Savini and re-cut for the Italian market by Dario Argento and re-scored by Goblin. I'm lucky enough to have seen the Italian version projected. Called *Wampyr*, it plays like a rock opera version of Murnau's *Nosferatu*. For the first quarter almost the only word heard is a repeated "Nosferatu" (not unlike the "kill' chants in *Suspiria*). Actually, the Italian cut plays wholly like a Dario Argento film, though Romero and his novice cinematographer, Michael Gornick, do not have the visual artistry of Argento and his camera teams. Argento starts the film with Martin and his uncle walking the streets together, and not with the slaughter in the train. This adds an edge of madness to the uncle and his repeated cries of "*Nosferatu*", and it makes Martin a more sympathetic character... until Martin's madness shows. *Martin* was one of the very first horror films to be positively reviewed in a mainstream English newspaper. David Robinson of *The Times* wrote that it was one of the best films in the world.

A chiller diller of a thriller... it's as grisly and frightening as anything you have paid money to see. Ivan Waterman, NEWS OF THE WORLD

Michael Winner knows how to provide the goods... shivering effects.. bravura fantasy Richard Barkley, SUNDAY EXPRESS

"Spectacular shock effects ...don't see it on a full stomach."
Arthur Thirkell, DAILY MIRROR

"Say your prayers before going and you may come out of the cinema undamaged."
Derek Malcolm, COSMOPOLITAN

"If your stomach stood up to 'The Exorcist', or enjoyed being turned on by it, you will probably thrill once more to the excesses of 'The Sentinel.'"
Nigel Andrews, FINANCIAL TIMES

"The dark shenanigans are eerie, unnerving and suspenseful. A smoothly-wrought shocker that rivets attention right up to the last reel."
Bruce Williamson, PLAYBOY

"Genuinely eerie."
Alan Brien, SUNDAY TIMES

"Devil-horror film addicts will love 'The Sentinel.'"
Kenneth Baily, SUNDAY PEOPLE

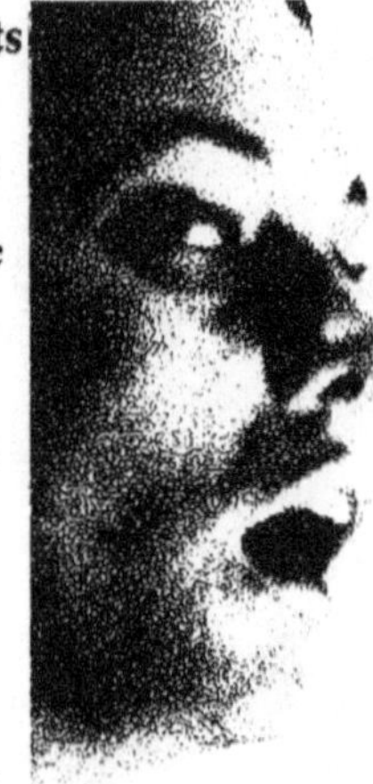

A MICHAEL WINNER FILM

"Michael Winner delivers his shock effects like a series of knowing jabs to the psyche, making nightmares come alive. The shocks are blood-freezers."
Gordon Gow, FILMS AND FILMING

"Michael Winner has pulled out all the stops... there are many shocks in this blood-curdler."
Roy Pickard, PHOTOPLAY

"Devilishly clever... good gruesome fun."
F. Maurice Speed, WHAT'S ON IN LONDON

"It is diabolically well-made. It pins you to your seat." Michael Billington, BIRMINGHAM POST

"Winner goes in for violent shocks to the nerve endings." Christopher Porterfield, TIME

"A neat, handsome and sub-acid job."
John Coleman, NEW STATESMAN

Diabolical...demented...guaranteed to make your skin crawl.
Jill Frankham, THE SUN

The Sentinel, 1977
d/p. Michael Winner

Rabid, 1977 d. David Cronenberg
p. John Dunning

Like all children growing up in 1970s Britain, the thing that scared me most was rabies, although rabies didn't exist in Britain. It had been eradicated centuries ago. That strange all-enveloping fear was the natural result of the government running a constant barrage of terrifying rabies adverts on children's television, backed up with posters on all the buses and trains. Warnings about wild dogs. Really harrowing stuff. If ever you were stupid enough to try to leave the island, the airports and ferry ports would greet you with black-and-red posters of rabid dogs barking with frothing mouths. We were told it was the most painful disease to have and we all knew about pain. The discomforts of childhood diseases were fresh with us. The playground shivered with the lasting urban legend that if you caught rabies you had to have eight injections in your stomach with a giant needle. Seventies Britain was basically one big David Cronenberg film.

When I was seven or eight years old, I remember shielding my eyes to be able to look through the glass of the pre-foyer room of the Savoy cinema in St. Helens, a 1,467 seater beauty with a wide curling staircase. When *Carrie* was playing, you could stand in the foyer and hear the patrons scream. Looking through the glass that day I saw an artist's easel on which was placed a framed poster for *Rabid*. It was the first time I had seen a photograph showing the effect of rabies on a human being. It was scarier than my own imagination. Though terrified, I left my parent's side again, that long slow morning of shopping, to go back to the Savoy and look again through the glass at that poster.

WE KILLED THEM IN KANSAS CITY...

April 7-8, '78

THEATRE	2 DAY GROSS
MEADOWLARK D.I. Wichita, Ks.	$ 3,871
FAIRLAND D.I. Kansas City, Mo.	4,800
SOUTH D.I. Olathe, Ks.	3,837
NORTH D.I. Riverside, Mo.	3,648
CREST D.I. Kansas City, Mo.	3,748
BELT D.I. St. Joseph, Mo.	3,873
71 D.I. Fayetteville, Ark.	3,573
TRI-STATE D.I. Joplin, Mo.	2,670
STATE D.I. Kansas City, Ks.	6,157
TWIN Independence, Mo.	5,750
COMMUNITY 917 Topeka, Ks.	4,250
SOUTH HUTCH D.I. Hutchinson, Ks.	2,581
WEEKEND TOTAL	$85,000 FIRST WEEK AND HOLDING

WE MURDERED THEM IN MINNEAPOLIS...

April 14-16, '78

THEATRE	3 DAY GROSS
Lucky	$ 4,348
Starlite	5,013
Coral	5,969
Rose	6,641
Sioux Falls	3,530
Coon Rapids	4,027
St. Croix	4,915
St. Cloud	3,687
Bismarck	2,619
France	3,499
Wilmar	1,304
Worthington	1,272
Watertown	1,661
Eau Claire	3,414
WEEKEND TOTAL	$51,899

★ AND WE'RE ONE OF THE FEW INDEPENDENT PICTURES GETTING BOOKINGS

ST. LOUIS, MISSOURI	APRIL 26, 50 Theatres
DENVER	MAY 3, 30 Theatres
BOSTON—NEW HAVEN	MAY 17, 60 Theatres
CLEVELAND, OHIO	MAY 12, 40 Theatres
WASHINGTON, D.C.	MAY 17, 25 Theatres
PITTSBURGH, PENNSYLVANIA	JUNE, 42 Theatres

ALSO, GROSSING WELL THE SECOND TIME AROUND

AT CANNES MAY 14-22
Montfleury Intercontinental Hotel
(93) 689150

NATIONAL DISTRIBUTOR
VANGUARD RELEASING INC.
8831 Sunset Blvd.
Los Angeles, Ca 90069
(213) 652-2630
CONTACT: BARRY CAHN and PETER LOCKE

SUB-DISTRIBUTORS —

New York — New England
CINEMA SHARES INTL. DIST.
450 Park Ave.
New York, NY 10022
(212) 421-3371

Western States:
FAR WEST FILMS
116 No. Robertson
Los Angeles, Ca 90048
(213) 659-5161

Detroit — Cleveland
C. J. RUFF FILM DIST.
23300 Greenfield Rd.
Oak Park, Mich. 48237
(313) 968-7770

Cincinnati-Indianapolis
C. J. RUFF FILM DIST.
1620 Harrison Avenue
Cincinnati, Ohio 45214
(513) 921-8200

Charlotte:
DOMINANT PICTURES
230 S. Tryon St.
Charlotte, NC 28202
(704) 334-1391

New Orleans:
SOUTHERN FILM DISTRIBUTING CORP.
1821 Airline Hwy.
Metairie, La 70004
(504) 837-5200

Dallas
DAL-ART FILM EXCHANGE
2017 Young St
Dallas, Texas 75201
(214) 748-8342

Minneapolis:
ASSOCIATED FILM DISTRIBUTORS, LTD.
704 Hennepin Ave., #225
Minneapolis, Minn. 55403
(612) 332-3303

Philadelphia —Washington, D.C.
MAGILL FILMS, INC.
1612 Market St
Philadelphia, Pa. 19103
(215) 563-7428

Canada
ASTRAL FILMS LTD.
224 Davenport Rd
Toronto, Canada
(416) 364-3894

Chicago—Milwaukee:
SK FILMS, INC.
32 W. Randolph Ave
Chicago, Ill. 60601
(312) 236-2419
236-2420

Atlanta — Jacksonville:
NEW WORLD PICTURES OF ATLANTA
2200 Century Pkwy., Suite 390
Atlanta, Ga 30345
(404) 321-2910

Pittsburgh:
NEW WORLD PICTURES OF PITTSBURGH
29001 Cedar Rd., Suite 451
Lyndhurst, Ohio 44124
(216) 461-9770

Kansas City — St. Louis — Des Moines — Omaha:
THOMAS & SHIPP FILMS, INC.
110 West 18th St.
Kansas City, Mo 64108
(816) 421-1692

The Hills Have Eyes, 1977 d. Wes Craven p. Peter Locke

This 1978 trade ad for Wes Craven's fine film about a family holiday contains a lot of impressive information and statistics but the strong strange image of the dome-headed Michael Berryman still stands out. In time, the image would jump from a million newspapers as *Hills* played the drive-in circuit and the multi-bill repertory cinemas for more than a decade.

Alice, Sweet Alice aka
Holy Communion aka...,
1976
d/p. Alfred Sole

Piranha, 1978
d. Joe Dante
p. Roger Corman

A neurosurgeon fuses his crash-damaged son with a prototype racing car that's wired to his brain. In addition to preserving imagery from lost films that were filmed, the press advert is sometimes the only visual artifact for a film that was scripted but not made. The unfilmed *Frankencar* was written for *Death Race 2000* mastro, Paul Bartel, by Richard Blackburn, who had directed *Lenora* (1973).

Halloween, 1978 d. John Carpenter p. Debra Hill

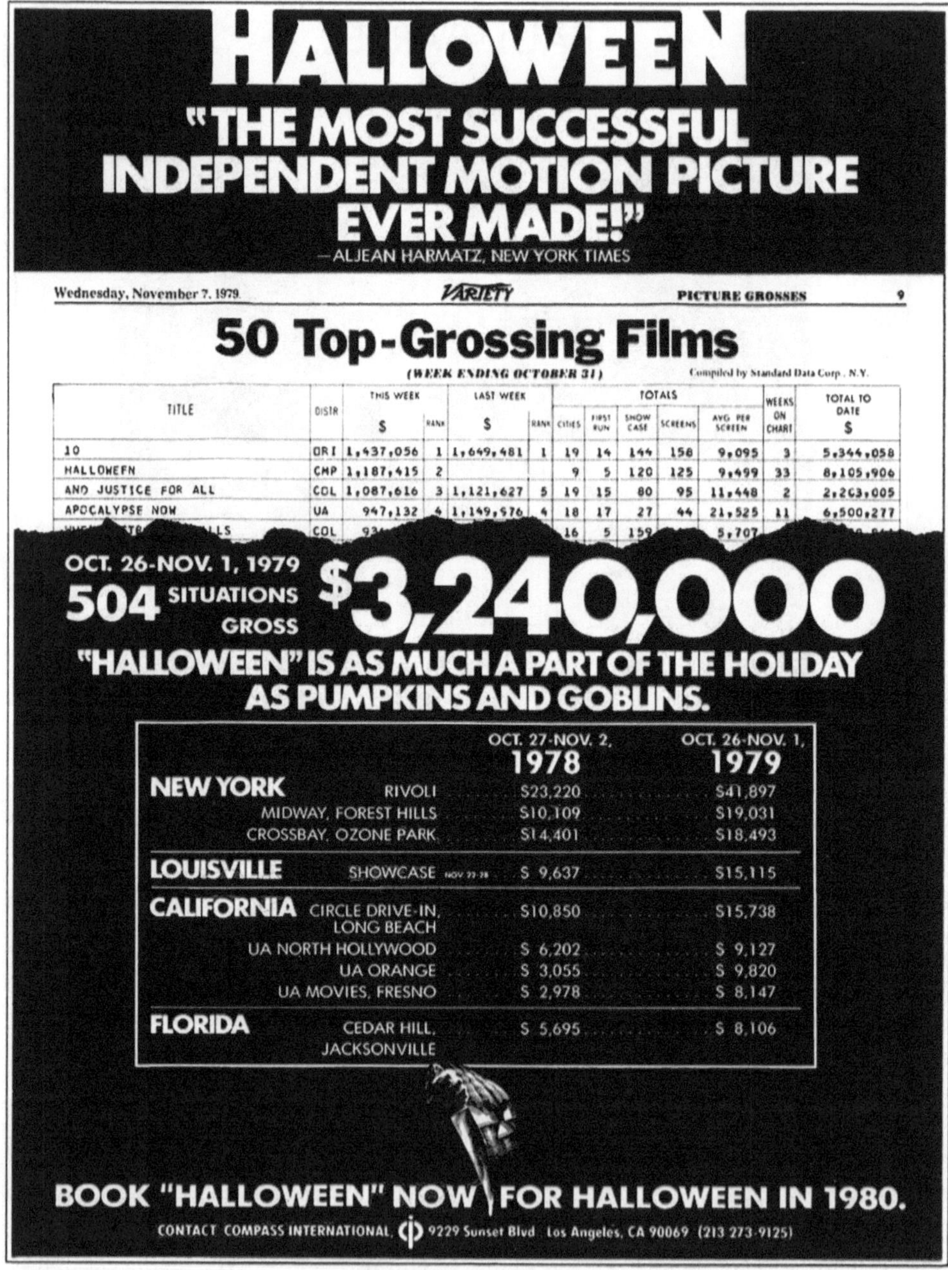

Wednesday, November 7, 1979. *VARIETY* PICTURE GROSSES 9

50 Top-Grossing Films
(WEEK ENDING OCTOBER 31) Compiled by Standard Data Corp., N.Y.

TITLE	DISTR	THIS WEEK $	RANK	LAST WEEK $	RANK	CITIES	FIRST RUN	SHOW CASE	SCREENS	AVG PER SCREEN	WEEKS ON CHART	TOTAL TO DATE $
10	ORI	1,437,056	1	1,649,481	1	19	14	144	158	9,095	3	5,344,058
HALLOWEFN	CMP	1,187,415	2			9	5	120	125	9,499	33	8,105,906
AND JUSTICE FOR ALL	COL	1,087,616	3	1,121,627	5	19	15	80	95	11,448	2	2,263,005
APOCALYPSE NOW	UA	947,132	4	1,149,576	4	18	17	27	44	21,525	11	6,500,277
	COL	934				16	5	159		5,707		

	OCT. 27-NOV. 2, 1978	OCT. 26-NOV. 1, 1979
NEW YORK RIVOLI	$23,220	$41,897
MIDWAY, FOREST HILLS	$10,109	$19,031
CROSSBAY, OZONE PARK	$14,401	$18,493
LOUISVILLE SHOWCASE NOV 22-28	$ 9,637	$15,115
CALIFORNIA CIRCLE DRIVE-IN, LONG BEACH	$10,850	$15,738
UA NORTH HOLLYWOOD	$ 6,202	$ 9,127
UA ORANGE	$ 3,055	$ 9,820
UA MOVIES, FRESNO	$ 2,978	$ 8,147
FLORIDA CEDAR HILL, JACKSONVILLE	$ 5,695	$ 8,106

Pound for pound, *Halloween* was the most financially successful independent film of all-time, and remained so until nudged from the top spot by another horror film - *The Blair Witch Project* (1999)

CINEMA WEST
355-4451
II. 7:45-9:25
LOW PRICES! ADMISSION ONLY $2.50
R
HELD OVER! 5th SMASH WEEK!
HE CAME HOME FOR
HALLOWEEN

BOULEVARD ADULT DRIVE-IN
Biscayne Blvd. & 143rd St.
3 X-RATED FEATURES!
"HOOKERS CONVENTION"
plus
"PSYCHIATRIST"
and
"SWINGING PUSSYCATS"

GALA TWIN
BIRD RD. & 87 AVE. 226-0914
LOW PRICES!
ACADEMY WINNERS
JON VOIGHT — JANE FONDA
1 R Coming Home
2 IT'S BACK TO THRILL YOU R
"HALLOWEEN"

HALLOWEEN
The Night He Came Home!
NOTE! HALLOWEEN IS FULL OF THE KINDS OF THINGS THAT MAKE UP THE SCARIEST OF NIGHTMARES
DON'T SEE IT ALONE!
PANAVISION METROCOLOR A COMPASS INTERNATIONAL RELEASE
R RESTRICTED
NOW PLAYING
CHECK MOVIE TIME CLOCK FOR FEATURE TIMES
SUNILAND TWIN
11993 S. DIXIE HWY.
233-2540
GABLES
3113 PONCE DE LEON, C.G.
446-4621
RIO DRIVE-IN
233 NE 1 AV.
371-0706
27TH AVE. DRIVE-IN
2700 NW 87TH ST.
691-6934
GALA TWIN THEATRE
BIRD RD. & 87TH AVE.
226-0914
FLORIDA TWIN
HOLLYWOOD MALL
987-0350

Trick Or Treat Comes One Night Early!
HALLOWEEN
FIRST TIME ON TV!
4,13
9:00PM While all the children are tricking or treating, a psycho is on the loose. From the man who terrified you with "Prom Night" and "The Fog."
Jamie Lee Curtis • Donald Pleasence
Parental Discretion Advised

SNEAK PREVIEW TONIGHT
OF THE SHOCK THRILLER OF THE YEAR
R RESTRICTED
DUKE
1605 CHESTNUT ST
563-9881
SEE 2 FEATURES!
SNEAK PREVIEW AT 9:15 P.M.
"KING OF THE GYPSIES" — 11:20, 1:20, 3:20, 5:20, 7:20, 10:45
SNEAK PREVIEW AT THESE THEATRES AT 8 P.M.
ERIC TWIN HORSHAM
Blair Mill Rd. & Moreland Ave.,
Horsham, Pa.
ERIC TWIN KING
1 mi N. of Sch. Exp, Rt
King of Prussia, Pa.
ERIC TWIN PENN JERSEY
Rt. 1 at Olds Blvd.,
Fairless Hills, Pa.
NEW JERSEY
ERIC TWIN LAWRENCEVILLE
US 1 nr Texas Ave.,
Lawrenceville, N. J.
ERIC 3 PENNSAUKEN
Rts 73 & 130 nr. Tac Br.
Pennsauken, N. J.
DELAWARE
ERIC 3 TRI-STATE MALL
I-95, Naamans Rd.,
Claymont, Del.
SEE DIRECTORY FOR REGULAR FEATURE AND SHOW TIMES

HALLOWEEN
The Night He Came Home!
READ THE BANTAM BOOK
SPECIAL MIDNITE SHOW! TONITE ONLY AT MIDTOWN AND SELECTED AREA THEATRES
MOUSTAPHA AKKAD PRESENTS DONALD PLEASENCE IN JOHN CARPENTER'S HALLOWEEN WITH JAMIE LEE CURTIS PJ SOLES NANCY LOOMIS WRITTEN BY JOHN CARPENTER AND DEBRA HILL EXECUTIVE PRODUCER IRWIN YABLANS DIRECTED BY JOHN CARPENTER PRODUCED BY DEBRA HILL
R RESTRICTED
STARTS TODAY! YOUR CHOICE OF PREVIEWS AT MIDTOWN
SEE 2 FEATURES • DOORS OPEN 11:45 A.M.
BUDCO MIDTOWN 1
CHESTNUT at BROAD 567-7021
(COME AS LATE AS 10:20 PM & SEE 2 FEATURES)
"HALLOWEEN" 1:40, 5:05, 8:35, 12 MIDNITE
"MOTHER'S DAY" 12:00, 3:25, 6:50, 10:15
FREE BOOK! "HALLOWEEN" TO FIRST 250 PATRONS AT MIDTOWN ONLY
BUDCO MIDTOWN 2
CHESTNUT at BROAD 567-7021
(COME AS LATE AS 9:30 PM & SEE 2 FEATURES)
"HALLOWEEN" 12:15, 3:55, 7:40, 11:20
"EXTERMINATOR" 2:05, 5:45, 9:30
"HALLOWEEN" ONLY—ALSO STARTS TODAY AT THESE SELECTED AREA THEATRES
AMC PREMIERE*
Rt. 1 & Pa. Tpk.
BUDCO ANDORRA TWIN
Ridge & Henry Aves.
BUDCO BARN 5
1½ Miles S. of Doylestown
BUDCO CITY LINE TWIN
77th & City Line Ave
BUDCO EXTON D/I
Rts. 30 & 100, Exton
BUDCO ORLEANS 4
Cottman & Bustleton N.E. Phila
BUDCO 61ST STREET D/I*
On 61st above Passyunk, Perry's Corner
BUDCO SPRINGFIELD TWIN
Baltimore Pk. & Sproul Rd. Del. Co.
BUDCO 309 TWIN D/I*
End of 309 Expwy at Rt. 63, Montgomeryville
CHELTENHAM TWIN*
Cheltenham Shop. Ctr
TOWNE TWIN
Levittown Shop. Ctr. Rt. 13
NEW JERSEY
BUDCO COMMUNITY
Rt. 70, Barclay Farms Ctr
BUDCO MILLSIDE TWIN
Rt. 130, Delran
BUDCO PENNSAUKEN D/I*
Rt. 73-2 Miles from Tac. Pal. Bridge
SUPER 130 D/I
Rt. 130 S. of Willingboro
DELAWARE
BUDCO BRANMAR TWIN
Marsh & Silverside Rd., N. Wilm
NO MIDNITE SHOWS

The Brood, 1979 d. David Cronenberg p. Claude Héroux

Impressively original and articulate horror film starring the great Oliver Reed whose unique whisper-shout acting style, a powder-keg waiting to explode, seems to have informed the film's style and construction. From claustrophobic interiors to wide open spaces. From lulling whispers to shouts and screams the shape of rage. Alas, logic goes out of the window and Reed isn't given the chance to explode in the final showdown. Instead he's 'bundled' by a crowd of infants! There's a memorably focused and dark performance by young Cindy Hinds as the only child of Eggar born with a navel. Eggar herself is wild-eyed and bat-crazy with perfect diction, but her final monologue is compromised by being shot on lesser stock, or more likely printed from a cropped zoom. The grain dances.

Salem's Lot, 1978 d. Tobe Hooper p. Stirling Silliphant

A dodgy old Englishman imports antiques and a vampire into rural Maine but he hadn't reckoned on the arrival of ... a writer! (*Crash of thunder*). Stephen King got locked into a decades long rut of trying to forge a myth about The Writer as Action Hero. The only writer book to really hit home was the one about The Writer Villain (*Jack splinters the door with an axe*). *Salem's Lot's* assets are its length and its casting. Soul and Kerwin make for an attractively strong father and surrogate son; Mason, a suave and dangerous foreigner; Reggie Nalder, the bastard blue-faced son of Nosferatu. Good supporting cast too.

Nightwing, 1979 d. Arthur Hiller p. Martin Ransohoff

Invasion of the Body Snatchers, 1978
d. Philip Kaufman p. Robert H. Solo

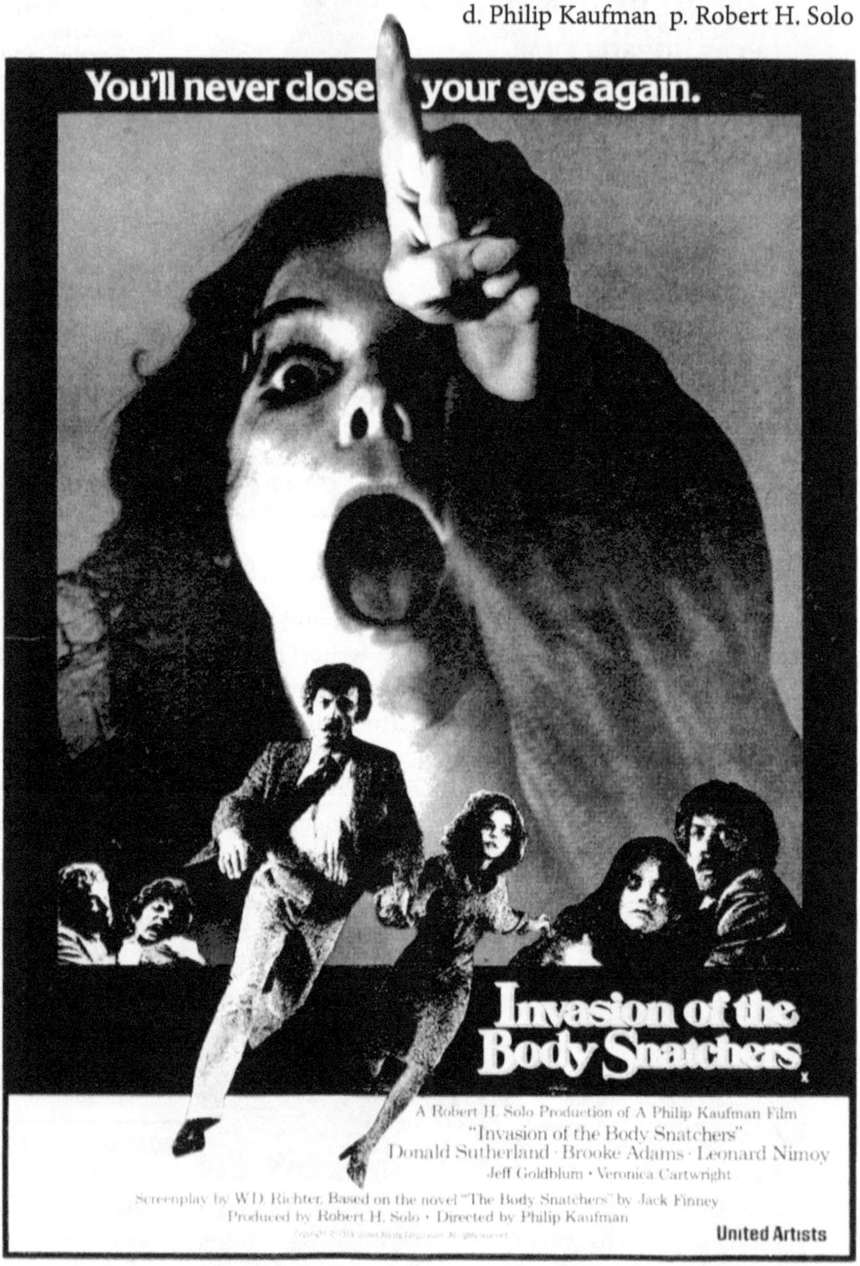

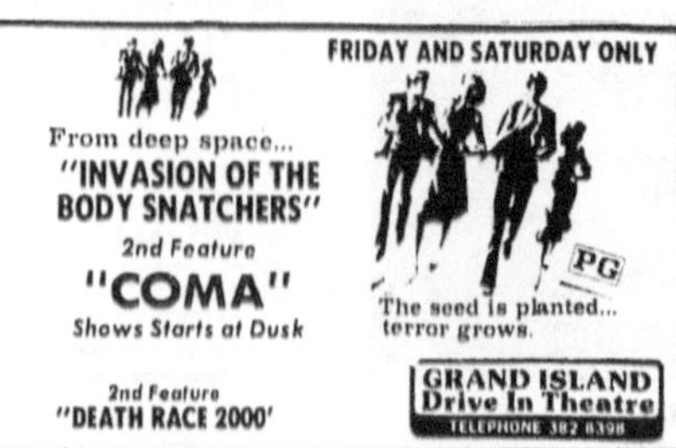

After spending a Cinecittà year having his strings pulled by Fellini and being forced to fall in love with a mannequin in *Casanova*, in which he gives one of the century's great performances, Donald Sutherland starred in this fine American film about the fight against conformity and doppelgangery.

Phantasm, 1979 d/p. Don Coscarelli

The macabre atmosphere is created and sustained by a good electronic score and by a unique air of incomprehensibility. The characters don't react as one would expect them to. Moments of gory horror, such as a flying steel ball drilling a hole in a man's head and draining him of blood (but leaving behind a pool of is-it-urine?) are met with a shrug as if it is all a dream which, of course, it is. We learn in the fresh and fascinating fourth film that these are the dreams of a dying boy. In his dreams, the boy is a motorbike riding, car-fixing, gun-shooting lad who has to escape from The Tall Man, a mortuary attendant who recycles the dead into midgets for use as slave labour on a red-sky planet in another dimension. The rhythm of the nightmare is set by repeated shots of the mortuary, by cross-cutting across scenes, and by each real-time *narrative* scene starting and finishing with an unsettling abruptness.

179

THE ZOMBIES ARE COMING IN 1978!

DARIO ARGENTO

PRESENTS A NEW ACTION THRILLER

DIRECTED BY **GEORGE A. ROMERO**

BASED ON HIS FORTHCOMING NOVEL "DAWN OF THE DEAD"
To be published by St. Martin's Press

PRODUCED BY **RICHARD RUBINSTEIN**
IN ASSOCIATION WITH
CLAUDIO ARGENTO AND ALFREDO CUOMO

THESE CREDITS NOT DEEMED TO BE CONTRACTUAL
©1977 DAWN ASSOCIATES

IN FUTURE SOUND
WHEN THERE'S NO MORE ROOM IN HELL... THE DEAD WILL WALK THE EARTH

USA, CANADA AND ENGLISH LANGUAGE TERRITORIES:
IRVIN SHAPIRO, FILMS AROUND THE WORLD, INC., NEW YORK

ALL OTHER TERRITORIES:
ROBERT LITTLE, TITANUS OVERSEAS, ROME

Dawn of the Dead, 1978 d. George A. Romero p. Richard Rubinstein, Dario Argento

For some reason the distributors think the are making an 'action thriller'.

Dawn of the Dead introduced a new type of money shot, a special effect served up with such élan that the audience instinctively applaud. Here a woman's arm bursts blood as it is ripped by a zombie's bite. It's *Grand Guignol* for the 20th Century. Fantastic movie magic by make-up pioneer, Tom Savini and by the lighting cameraman, Michael Gornick, and the director. The showpieces come mostly during the film's book-ends, two extended set-pieces of such exquisitely imaginative and well-crafted gore that we forgive the film its longeurs. Romero forgoes camera movement for a huge amount of set-ups and very quick cutting, as if he's making a two-hour version of the *Psycho* shower scene. Scene for scene the film is fast but the whole is rather slow. And I don't care. Because I like the actors, I like the setting and I like the show. The ad art is by Tom Chantrell, famed for his work with Hammer.

Tout Nouveau,
Jamais Vu !

Lorsqu'il n'y aura
plus de places en enfer,
les morts reviendront
sur terre...

ALERTE!

ZOMBIE LE
CRÉPUSCULE
DES MORTS VIVANTS

"DAWN of the DEAD"

29 FILM ASSAUT
COMMENÇANT VENDREDI À JEUDI

Attention: spectacle sur scène
jeudi 29 janvier

cinéma le paris

2380 ST-JOSEPH ST-HYACINTHE 773-9492

When there's no more room in HELL
the dead will walk the EARTH

First there was
'NIGHT OF THE
LIVING DEAD'

Now
GEORGE A.
ROMERO'S

PREMIERE
ENGAGEMENT
STARTS
TODAY

DAWN OF THE DEAD

Starring DAVID EMGE KEN FOREE SCOTT H. REINIGER GAYLEN ROSS Director of Photography MICHAEL GORNICK Music By THE GOBLINS with DARIO ARGENTO
Produced By RICHARD P. RUBINSTEIN Written and Directed by GEORGE A. ROMERO

GATEWAY   CINEMA WORLD   CINEMETTE EAST

Miércoles 20 de agosto terrorífico estreno
EL CID • UNICENTRO A • CHAPINERO 1

Prepárese para el más intenso e
increíble terror, espanto y violencia

Primero fue
"LA NOCHE DE LOS MUERTOS VIVOS"

ahora GEORGE A. ROMERO nos trae

ZOMBIE

COLOR

Los muertos se levantarán sedientos
de sangre de sus tumbas.

WENN IN DER HÖLLE
KEIN PLATZ MEHR IST
KOMMEN DIE TOTEN
AUF DIE ERDE ZURÜCK

George A. Romero's

ZOMBIE

Es gibt keinen härteren Film.

Constantin Film

presents MIDNIGHT MOVIES

92MJQ

TONIGHT AND SATURDAY AT MIDNIGHT!
SPEND THE HALLOWEEN WEEKEND
WITH US

Screen 1   Screen 2

FRIDAY THE 13TH
PART 2

BOTH MOVIES AT
BOTH THEATRES!

DAWN OF THE DEAD

JO-MOR'S
STONERIDGE TWIN
621-1550 RIDGE RD. W.

JO-MOR'S
PANORAMA TWIN
381-7880 PENFIELD RD.

Zombie Flesh Eaters, 1978 d. Lucio Fulci p. Fabrizio De Angelis

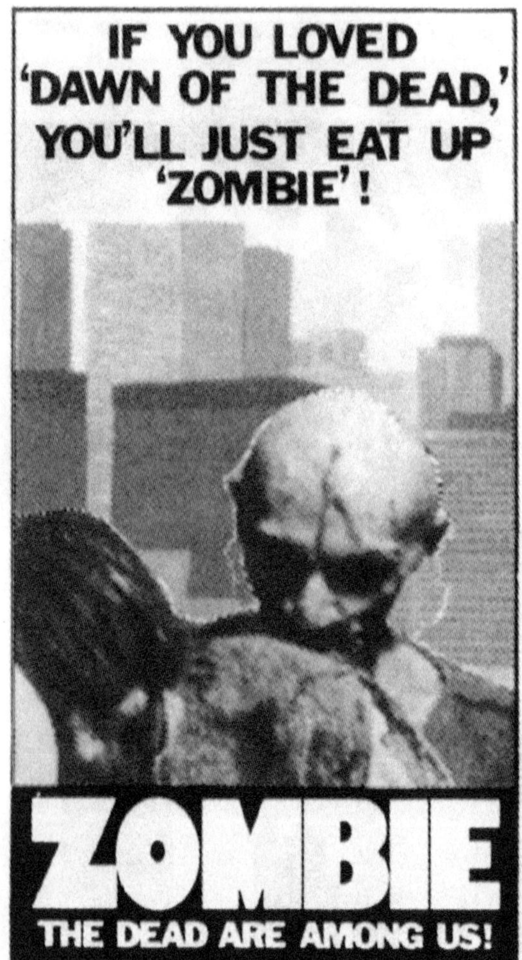

The bald head references the ad art for *Dawn of the Dead*. The collage suggests *Dawn's* fabulous neck bite showpiece. Curiously, *Zombie Flesh Eaters* was released in Britain before *Dawn of the Dead*, such was the feet-dragging of film distribution at the time. e.g. *E.T.* opened in the USA in May 1982 but didn't play in cinemas in the UK until December (or in the North West until 1983), i.e. long after video piracy had been forced to move to industrial levels to satisfy the public demand.

Zombie Flesh Eaters as the red meat on a 1981 triple-bill that played all over America.

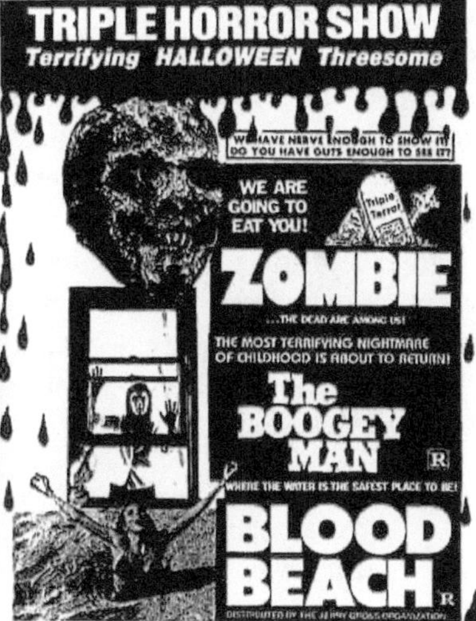

A starry film packed with in-
discriminate killing. It has a
shape-shifting 'alien' fought with
flamethrowers but which can't be
destroyed, a score by Jerry Gold-
smith, an inopportune birth scene
and a sirens-and-explosion finale.
A team of crack soldiers enter a
futuristic base but find everyone
dead except for a cold scientist, a
robotic-like Englishman who admits
to admiring the invader. Scott and
Cameron must have been watching.

The Swarm, 1978
d/p. Irwin Allen

The Amityville Horror, 1979 d. Stuart Rosenberg p. Samuel Z. Arkoff

The Driller Killer, 1979 d/p. Abel Ferrara

Filming in his own Manhattan apartment, Ferrara himself stars as an on-the-edge of poverty artist with his hopes pinned on finishing and selling a giant painting of a buffalo. Punk rock neighbours, rabbit stew, and an advert for a portable power pack, summon up the spirit that saw the West's first tenants drive the buffalo from the land. Or something like that. There's a dark energy and some powerful scenes in this flip-side to Woody Allen's *Manhattan,* made and released the same year. The print ads sparked a tidal wave of censorship in the UK.

And finally...

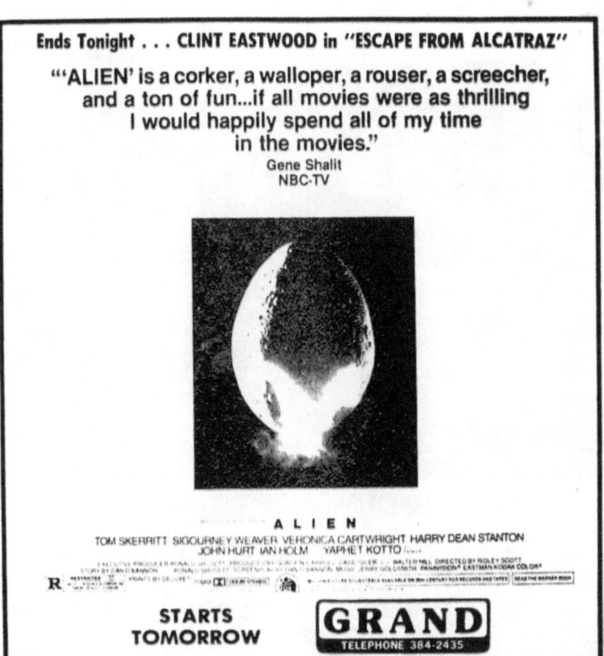

Ends Tonight . . . CLINT EASTWOOD in "ESCAPE FROM ALCATRAZ"

"'ALIEN' is a corker, a walloper, a rouser, a screecher,
and a ton of fun...if all movies were as thrilling
I would happily spend all of my time
in the movies."
Gene Shalit
NBC-TV

A L I E N

TOM SKERRITT SIGOURNEY WEAVER VERONICA CARTWRIGHT HARRY DEAN STANTON
JOHN HURT IAN HOLM   YAPHET KOTTO

STARTS
TOMORROW

GRAND
TELEPHONE 384-2435

Close Encounters of the Third King, 1977 d. Steven Spielberg p. J & M Phillips

A horror film? No, but included here because this advert certainly did inspire a horror ad masterpiece. This press ad for *CE3K* takes the basic shape and structure of the famous *Rosemary's Baby* poster, from which we got the poster of *Jaws*, and it adds 'the night', a mysterious glow, and a vanishing point highway suggestive of the landscapes in Jack Arnold's *It Came From Outer Space.*

Alien, 1979 d. Ridley Scott p. Gordon Carroll, David Giler, Walter Hill

Though advertised as a film about silent screaming, it starts with a lot of interesting noise. We hear screeching computers, bass rumbling engines, a heartbeat, breathing, a howling wind, dripping water, steam and sirens. From within this cathedral of sound a monster awakes, the likes of which we hadn't seen before. This beautiful film is very much more than the sum of its parts. And somehow, by a lucky twist of fate, all of that is successfully represented by a paint-dusted hen's egg garnished with a crack of *Close Encounters* light, and by those unsettling gaps in the tweaked-Futura font. Amazing.

As this microfiche grab shows, the pointed round of the alien egg, the new visual shorthand for terror, was not a million miles from the shark logo for Spielberg's *Jaws*. It's only a 'pinched egg' step up from the round bald head as madness as sported by Kurt Raab in *Tenderness of the Wolves* to the pinched bald head as terror that was Michael Berryman in *The Hills Have Eyes*. The continuing use of the 'egg head' as shorthand for cinematic terror is shown in these ads for Fulci's *City of the Living Dead* (1980) heading triple and quadruple bills with *Mausoleum* (1983), *Funeral Home* (1980) and *Night of the Zombies* (1981). Though the bald head these reference is less the pinched egg of *Alien* and more the about-to-be-cracked head of Romero's *Dawn of the Dead*.

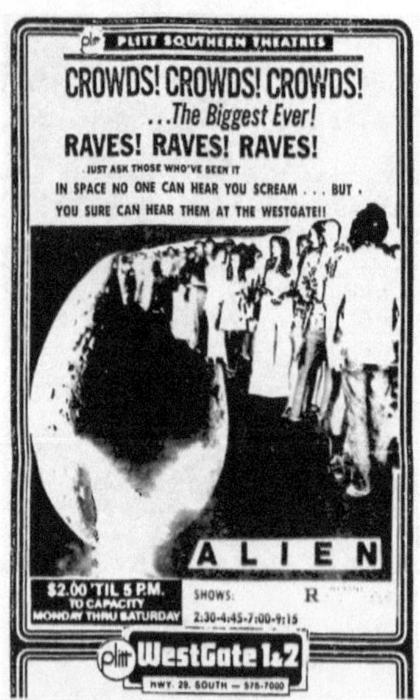

www.ingramcontent.com/pod-product-compliance
Lightning Source LLC
Chambersburg PA
CBHW022050050726
47591CB00002B/470